Lost & Found in Egypt

*A Most Unlikely Journey Through
the Shifting Sands of Love and Loss*

A Memoir

by

Kyla Merwin

Cover photo: An archway on the 3,750 Steps of Repentance, built by monks on the barren mountain, leading to the top of Mt. Sinai.

ISBN: 978-0-9910689-0-6
978-0-9910689-1-3 (e-book)

Published by
KMC Media Co.
Bend, Oregon

For Effie Agnes Desonia Morris (1913-1994)
and Terry Lee Fletter (1947-1994)
for smiling down on me from time to time
and for meeting me at the finish line.

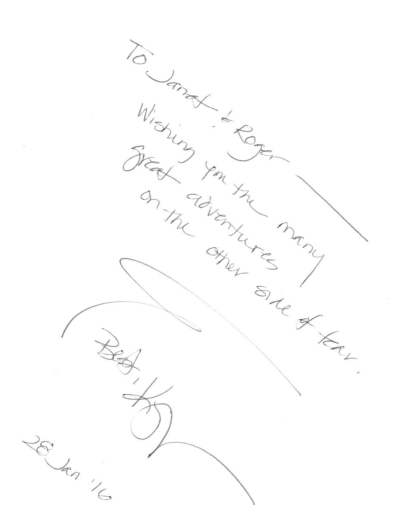

To Janet & Roger

Wishing you the many
great adventures
on the other side of fear.

Best, K

28 Jan '16

TABLE OF CONTENTS

PROLOGUE
EGYPT CALLS A WOMAN

THOTH: *Thoth is the god of words and numbers and the patron of scribes. He presides over the heart ceremony during burial rituals—where one's heart is weighed against the feather of truth to determine the weight of its sins. Thoth records the final verdict: whether the soul will ascend to eternity or be devoured by the waiting beast, Aman. Thoth is typically depicted in human form with the head of an ibis—a bird associated with the moon, and the measure of time. He holds an ankh, the emblem of life.*

I was the most unlikely woman in Egypt in the winter of 1999. Unlikely, unprepared, and under-funded. I didn't even have a hotel room when I arrived. The frenzied city of Cairo hit me like a jackhammer.

I had concocted this trip with a certain amount of *Lost Ark* bravado. I wanted to be a great adventurer and an important writer. When the trip actually came upon me, however, it scared the gumption out of me. I didn't want to go to Egypt alone. I was afraid of the many long flights that would take me nearly halfway across the globe. Afraid the Muslims would hate me because I was an *infidel*, a faithless one. Afraid of Osama Bin Laden, Yellow Fever, diarrhea, rape, torture, and land mines. Afraid of the ordinary people in a strange country. My mother worried that I'd be abducted into a harem, but I let that one go. Still, I was afraid. Two weeks before my departure, I drank an entire bottle of wine and sobbed myself to sleep. Still, I went.

That's when the trouble started. Smart travelers actually *plan* their trips: they make itineraries, day by day, with the appropriate tickets and reservations. I stuck my head in the sand and let the trip arrive without worrying about these mundane details. I didn't have a traveling visa or even a Visa card for that matter. When I stepped onto the Cairo-bound airplane, I had nothing more than some high-minded ideas about traipsing through the desert on my own, the phone number of the brother of a colleague of a friend, and four nights supposedly reserved at the Nile Hilton. The rest I would make up as I went.

Had I been prepared, I would have known that autumn is high season in Egypt. Savvy travelers avoid the blazing heat of Egyptian summers and opt for November instead. But I hadn't planned on that. Mine was the Get-There-and-Wing-It plan. At the most popular time of year, when everything was over-booked.

Even so, Egypt played a great role in my first novel and I had to see her for myself. I wanted to breathe the hot sandy air, touch the ancient stones, and watch the Nile slide silently by. I intended to plant myself firmly amongst the locals, buy food at open markets, ride ramshackle buses, hear the chants of the *muezzin* who call the Muslim to prayer, and watch the sun set over 6,000-year-old pyramids.

With ten places I *had* to see, two weeks of time, and not enough money to spend, I would call on Egypt. In her turn—with her demands and her offerings—Egypt would call on me.

Wide-eyed, I walked the streets of Cairo by myself: the chaotic downtown core, the enormous, open-air bazaar in old Cairo, the Christian museum in Coptic Cairo, and the mosques where Muslims go five times a day to pray in gratitude to God. Then I left on a bus and a prayer to the rural regions of Sinai, to climb the mountain of Moses on my own personal pilgrimage.

There was no mistaking me for a savvy traveler. At any given moment I would be lost, frightened, exhausted, or looking desperately for a place to pee.

I had the time of my life.

Traveling alone is different than living alone. Living in solitude, as I had for many years, like my grandfather and father before me, can harden a person. As can sameness. Loneliness had closed me up, like darkness and chill will cause a lily to fold in upon itself. At dawn, though, that same flower stretches herself toward the sun, recreating herself. Travel can be like that: the promise of dawn. The promise of change.

As a lone traveler, far from home, I opened myself up, I offered myself to strangeness. I stepped out the door of my hotel, past the guard with a machine gun slung over his shoulder, and onto the streets crowded with people who belonged there. I carried my backpack, my courage and my curiosity. And a 35mm camera.

Walking along next to me was Vulnerability. She was naked again— sometimes blithe, sometimes wary, and always likely to step straight into harm's way. On the other side of me, keeping pace, was Trust. She's a wacky, madcap kind of woman who just knows things. And she knows that she knows them. She's quieter than most. But she's there.

The three of us stepped out together and met what came our way.

Something began to happen on those thin sidewalks between fear and confidence, in a culture that was different, where the rules were re-written. Slowly, outside the familiar, I was invited to shed my everyday habits and expectations, and I began to change.

If I was the most unlikely of women in Egypt that autumn, and the most disorganized, I was also the most blessed. Every time I was in trouble, every single time, someone emerged from the chaos to help me. Or to comfort me, or welcome me, or embrace me. I consider one of these people a model of friendship. Others I never even knew their names. In one desperate instance, someone unexpected inside myself muscled herself forward to solve an unhappy problem. (Note: you can—even if you're a middle-aged woman with a desk job—bribe a tour bus operator on the Sinai peninsula. You can.)

Research offered me a tidy expedition—one of purpose, one that enjoyed the comforts of detachment and intellectual objectivity. I'd traveled alone before, plenty, in America. To the Washington coast, southern California, Sedona, Arizona and uncounted round trips between Montana and Oregon. To cabins and cottages and campgrounds. One of my favorite things to do is get in my car with my dog, a map and a suitcase, and drive somewhere. Always exploring, searching, traveling through the rough and scattered landscapes of my mind, trying to figure out who I am in this life.

This trip was supposed to be different. I would leave myself and my problems half a globe away.

It was not to be. I took my first step off the empirical highway of historical research when I walked out of the Cairo airport. I peered into the underground parking lot at 9 P.M. wondering, *Where is that man going with my suitcase? Should I follow? Should I run in the opposite direction?* Since I left home I had been lied to, cheated, propositioned, and hung over. And that was before I landed in Cairo. Now, a more tenacious road lay ahead of me. In Egypt's land of immortality, I found myself on a new path, relying on instincts I didn't know I had.

I didn't realize it until I got there, but I went to Egypt to run away from sorrow. A few years past, a dear, sweet, lovely man I knew, named Terry, had walked into his garage, put a yellow nylon chord around his neck and jumped off a cooler into eternity. I was wild with grief. For five years I hunkered down and took the blame upon myself. Egypt, for me, represented a great battlefield of reconciliation. But I didn't understand that until years later.

This is the truth as best as I remember it. The capital "T" Truth, however, remains a mystery to me. I can never see my life objectively. But I like to think that soulful things are happening below the surface, parallel to my outward struggles; that great wrongs are being righted on some universal playing field, that my struggles are payments, and I'm wiping sins off the slate of my life.

I might as well admit it: I went to Egypt to find what I'd been searching for, for a very long time. I went to Egypt to find God.

At 40 years old, I was defined by my wanderings. I couldn't stay in one place. I hadn't gotten around to getting married or having children. I didn't own a home. I'd made money, lost money, and turned my back on the great money machine of corporate servitude. I lived in a little apartment in a small town in the dead center of Oregon and ran a grassroots environmental organization. And Terry was dead.

My grief carried such a singular intensity, that I when I look back upon it, years later, I see it as strangely beautiful—in a passionate, bruised, broken-hearted sort of way. But in the thick of it, there was no beauty. There was no beginning and no end. There was only sadness—endless, billowing, dark clouds of grief.

When Terry killed himself, I thought I should be dead, too. I thought it was my fault. I never should have left him. Not as his girlfriend. Not ever alone. What kind of world was this all of a sudden, without him in it? Why stay? Terry and I were soul mates, weren't we? Two halves of the same whole. Our destinies were intertwined. Weren't they? He was born in 1947 and died when he was 47 years old. I was born in 1959. Would I die when I was 59?

Every day, something on my body came from Terry's closet, as if I could wear him back again. I thought if I cried enough, and waited enough, and wore my penance on my back enough, he would return to me and to the land of the living. I wore baggy shirts mostly, and sweaters, and around my neck I wore his bronze star from Vietnam, which his family passed over when they rifled through his dresser drawers. HEROIC OR MERITORIOUS ACHIEVEMENT, it reads. I wore it on a gold chain, every day for years, relying on it for the courage I needed. I also pretty much lived in his green silk bomber jacket. The one that I wore threadbare. The one that hangs in my closet 19 years later, as limp and empty as I felt at the time.

My then boyfriend, Chris, decided that if I was so torn up over Terry, I couldn't possibly love him. Or love him enough. So he dumped me on the night of Terry's funeral and went full-steam-ahead in pursuit of my best friend. She loved him back. After a wild romantic weekend in San Francisco and a few weeks of domesticity, however, reality set in and she went back to her husband. Everyone goes out on a limb for love now and then. Both of them are friends to me to this day, and, ironically, strangers to each other.

At the time, though, I sunk further. Under a dark, lonely blanket of despair, I saw no light and no reprieve. I began to entertain thoughts of joining Terry, wherever he was. I must have known, though, somewhere in a little hotspot in the back of my brain, that my grief would eventually pass. That every breath wouldn't hurt any more. That I would wake up from the nightmare and see beauty in the world again.

All beauty and hope had gone dark for Terry, though. Things had gone wrong for him, one after the other. He lost his business, then his job, his girlfriend, his happiness. A festering case of Post Traumatic Stress Disorder, financial straits, terrible loneliness, and a regular chardonnay habit, and that was the end of this man's life. The glorious, beautiful, bright, witty, magnificent life of Terry Lee Fletter—the King of the Fun Hogs—abruptly ended. As I knew it, so did mine.

I started to write. The local newspaper published my first essay, "When All the Laughter Died in Sorrow." At the end of the article, the byline read, "Kyla Merwin is a Bend writer." I fell to my knees on the spot and cried. From beyond the world of beating hearts, Terry had reached into my life and changed it. I was a writer. It said so in the newspaper.

So I began a life of writing. Now I'm ready to tell the story, these many years later, of the perfect storm of disappointments, losses, hopes and dreams that led me to Egypt. This is how I came to a journey of exploration and redemption and—as the ancient Egyptians had found—a life renewed.

Chapter One

Stranded: The First Knight

HATHOR: *Hathor is the daughter of the sun god, Ra, the goddess of joy and love, and the protector of women and travelers. She is depicted wearing cow horns, between which sits the solar disk. She also wears a manait, the symbol of joy and pleasure.*

All I wanted was a hot shower and ten solid hours of sleep. When the last of my flights touched Egyptian earth, I nearly wept from relief. I absolutely hate to fly and sometimes I swear I'm holding the plane up in the air through sheer will. I imagine many terrifying versions of fiery, dismembering deaths, falling at sharp, doomed pitches through 30,000 feet of sky. Every bump, turn and noise ignites the worst of predictions. But four planes, 36 hours, 10 time zones and three countries from Saturday night, had finally brought me to the city of my obsession: Cairo.

I worried that I might be sent immediately back home, because I didn't have a traveling visa for Egypt. I stood in line at Passport Control with all the confident people and sweated bullets. Fifteen dollars later, plus a stamp in my blue passport, I stepped through the iron gateway. I was in Cairo. Exhausted, hungry, and nervous, but I was there.

This is when things started going wrong. An official-looking Egyptian with a photo ID card clipped to his gray suit stepped forward the moment I had passed through Passport Control. "Welcome to Egypt," he said with a warm smile. "Is this your first time in Cairo?"

This exact same thing happened to me in Mexico seven years later. I gave that guy the buzz-off savvy traveler attitude of someone who knows a timeshare scam when she sees one. "I'm staying with friends," I said (a total lie) and walked away.

But I had no friends and no such shrewdness in Cairo. "Thank you," I said. "Yes, it is."

"Where are you from?"

"Canada." I'd been told to lie about being an American. It seems terrorists don't mind our kinder, gentler neighbors to the north.

"Where in Canada?"

"Uh..." *Quebec?* No. I had been to Victoria once, and I remember thinking that they speak French in Quebec. "I'm from Victoria."

"Welcome! Welcome!" He shook my hand. "My name is Jamil. I'm with the Egyptian Tourist Department. Welcome to our country." Travelers buzzed all around us with intention and purpose. They wore turbans, and long robes called *jallabayas,*and scarves, and business suits, and they spoke Arabic. It was simultaneously exhilarating and intimidating. They talked on cell phones, greeted relatives, toted briefcases and moved through the airport with the simple self-assurance of people on familiar ground.

The terra firma below me, however, was an undulating sea of the strange and unfamiliar. "Thank you," I said, and moved with the crowd toward baggage claim. Jamil strode beside me step for step. While I waited for my suitcase, he continued to welcome and encourage and instruct me, offering me advice on places to stay and things to do. "What's your name, again?" I asked.

"Jamil." He pointed to his badge. "You can call me Jamie, though. It's easier. What does your suitcase look like?"

"Well, it's green, with little pink flowers. It's made out of fabric. Cloth." I rubbed my fingers together to illustrate. I suddenly noticed that I was the only traveler in baggage claim with my own personal private guide from the Egyptian Tourist Department.

"Where are you staying in Cairo?" he asked.

"The Nile Hilton."

Jamil blithely explained how he would call the Hilton shuttle for me, but sometimes it didn't come, but in that case he would call me a taxi for 35 Egyptian pounds. And while we waited he would give me some information—information I couldn't get anywhere else—regarding different tours and excursions for my stay in his beautiful country.

Three fibs right off the bat. One: the Hilton doesn't have an airport shuttle. Two: cab fare from the airport to the hotel costs about 20 Egyptian pounds. Three: roughly five zillion different tour companies operate in this city of 20 million people whose economy depends largely on tourism, any one of which would happily organize my stay in their beautiful country.

Jamil snatched up my luggage when it toddled by on the conveyor belt and guided me—with amazing speed—through Customs. In fact, we seemed to side-step Customs entirely, slipping through a break in the gateway and around the corner. Bewildered and confused, I raced to keep up. *This guy had my luggage.* Next, I found myself standing in front of the lighted booth of a tour company, with Jamil introducing me warmly to his manager. "This is Kyla, from Canada. This is her first time in Egypt."

"Hello. Welcome," said the manager. "We can help you."

"Hi." I shook his hand. "I really just want a cab to the Hilton."

"We'll call you the shuttle, don't worry," Jamil piped in. "Just wait five minutes."

This would be the phantom shuttle he was referring to. "No, really." I might be in a turbulent sea of the unfamiliar, with sleep deprivation and a hangover, but I was absolutely clear about this one thing:

"I want a cab to my hotel. That is all." I longed obsessively to check into my safe little hotel room, drink a glass of wine and sleep until the new day woke me.

"But you can't get the tour information in the city. Only here."

"I need to find a cab," I said, looking around for the exit. *Fish or cut bait.* That's what my grandmother would have said. *Enough now.* I started to move away from the tour booth.

"Here, here," Jamil raised his arm and called to a bone-thin man who rapidly approached us. They spoke for a moment in Arabic and then Jamil introduced him as my taxi driver. I was handed off, just that smoothly, and led out of the terminal.

"Twenty pounds," I said. "To take me to the Nile Hilton." I knew this was a fair rate.

"No, 35 pounds. It is a long way. A very long way."

I still needed to exchange my American dollars for Egyptian pounds. "No problem," said the taxi driver. "Do you have 10 American dollars?"

Ten dollars for what I knew to be a half-hour cab ride seemed reasonable. Much later I did the math on that: 34 Egyptian pounds. I hated being hustled. I would hate it again and again.

Outside the terminal, the driver began to lead me away from the main road and down a dark, curving driveway. He had my suitcase and I'd seen way too many movies involving underground parking garages and hapless females.

"Wait a second! Where are we going?"

"The car is down here," he assured me. "In parking."

Well, he has the heavy suitcase and I can always bolt the other way if I need to. I followed him down and around the ramp in the dark. I was learning, though I didn't know it then, when to follow, when to speak up, when to trust.

We eventually arrived at a van with the tour company's name printed on the side. This was a relief to me, and should have made me calm. But I had this penetrating fear of being abducted into the desert, and wouldn't relax until I was in my own room at the Hilton.

But first I had to take the Van-Ride-from-Hell into Cairo. I had never been so sure of my imminent demise. *How could they drive so fast and reckless through so much other fast and reckless traffic, and not all die?* It took twenty minutes of white knuckling to get to the Hilton. It never occurred to me to say, *Hey could you slow down a bit?* I wasn't raised that way.

Finally, finally, at 9:30 at night, after unimaginable imaginings of frightful, exploding collisions of traffic and thanking a merciful God in heaven above, I stood at the reservation counter at the Nile Hilton.

"Name?"

"Merwin, Kyla Merwin."

Tap-tap-tap on the computer.

I remember thinking that the hotel employee was very handsome: perfect teeth, dark hair, skin and eyes, with fabulous eyelashes. I began to wander in my thoughts. *Can good looks elevate one's position in Egyptian life? Why not? Aren't the lucky and the beautiful always intertwined?*

"Your name again, please."

"Kyla Merwin. M-E-R-W-I-N."

Tap-tap-tappety-tap. "Your passport please."

Every time I was asked for my passport I had to reach up under my sweater and unzip it from my super-secret, hidden money-belt, which Those-In-The-Know insisted I wear.

Tap-tap-tap.

Eyelash Man at the reservation counter said something in Arabic to the manager on duty, who came to look over his shoulder.

Tap-tap-tap.

"When did you make your reservation?"

"About a week ago." I knew exactly what was happening.

"Who made it for you?"

"Mt. Bachelor Travel Service in Bend, Oregon. In America." As if that would help.

"Do you have a confirmation number?"

Damn. How did I forget *that* little mundane detail? "No. . . I don't."

Tap-tap-tap.

"We don't have your name here," he said finally. "So sorry."

Let's cut to the chase, I thought. "Well, do you have a *room?*"

"No. The hotel is sold out. So sorry."

"You don't have a room? Not one tiny little room, somewhere in this big hotel?"

"No." Again he asked, "You don't have a confirmation number?"

"No, but I'll get one." I didn't have a room, but I had a plan. My best hope was to reach my sometimes boyfriend, Mike, immediately, who could call his agent at Mt. Bachelor Travel, and email back my confirmation number. "Where can I access the Internet?"

"At the Business Center, that way." Eyelash Man pointed. He handed me back my passport. "So sorry."

"Thank you." I might be miserable and homeless, but I was raised to be polite, dammit.

During the 30-second walk to the Business Center I started to cry. Shaking from the inside all the way out to a tiny voice, I asked the man behind the counter for access to email. "Yes. Thirty one and a half pounds for a half an hour."

That's about nine bucks. "No problem," I said, although I still had no Egyptian money.

Staving off a full-on sob fest, I plopped down in a chair in front of their computer. "Can you connect me to the internet?" I asked.

"Internet . . . Internet . . ." He leaned over my shoulder and clicked around *Yahoo!* for a few minutes. He had no idea. A woman walked in just then, from Canada she said (and I believed her), and asked if there was more than one computer terminal.

"Please to show email?" asked the man.

Five minutes later I had my own Hotmail account and could send and receive messages all over the world. "And, by the way," she whispered, "Don't come back here. There's a cyber cafe in the mall next door. Six pounds for half an hour." That's about two bucks.

I extended my thanks to this woman, who really was from Canada, who materialized at exactly the right moment. She came in the business office to get something she needed, and left only with my gratitude.

I typed my message to Mike, Subject: *Urgent from Cairo*. Words make things real. Writing somehow unlocks the barriers of propriety and my quietly leaking tears suddenly started racing each other down my face. *I'm off to a rough start*, I wrote. There it was. The truth. Not The Truth. But how could I know that? I was off to a rough start. I flat-out bawled into the keyboard.

Mike, I realized, was in Seattle at that very moment. Blackberrys hadn't been invented yet, and he wouldn't be checking his email for days and days. He was—as signified our relationship at the time—unreachable. I sent another *Urgent from Cairo* email to my girlfriend Brenda, listing Mike's cell and work numbers, in the hope that she would get my message to him, and he would email back to me the magic key to my hotel room.

This was my best plan, and it was worthless. I understood in that moment why people have international cell phones. At that time in my life, however, I still had a rotary dial telephone by my bed in Bend. The importance of technology in a modern world had yet to dawn on me.

I had done all I could do about my room at the Hilton. Game over. I unwrapped a leftover cookie from my backpack, ate it, and blew my nose in the paper napkin.

"Thank you," I said to the man in the Business Center, collecting myself to leave.

"Thirty-one and a half pounds, please."

"Oh, right. I have don't have Egyptian currency."

Not a problem. He pointed to a bank down the hall. "Right over there. Open 24 hours."

I returned 10 minutes later with gads of Egyptian money, exchanged at one American dollar for 3.41 Egyptian pounds, less a transaction fee. I unwittingly tried to pay the man with a 50 piaster bill—about 15 cents. "No," he said. "Excuse me." I held out my whole wad of money to him. "Here, and here, and here." He gingerly pointed to the bills that added up to thirty-one and a half pounds. Bill settled.

"The Business Center will re-open at 7 A.M.," he said, locking the door behind him. "You can come back then."

Bad news has a way of multiplying. What was I going to do for the next nine hours? Would they let me sleep sitting up in the lobby? No. I went back to the reservation desk and told them I was getting my confirmation number, and, could I leave my bag with the bell captain? "You don't have a room?" the new guy asked. "No, but I'm getting it worked out. Over email. *Email.*" I typed it out with my fingers. He had no idea.

"You are not a guest here?"

"Not yet. I'm working on it. The hotel lost my reservation..."

No room, no luggage. Take it with you. So sorry.

"Thank you." Dammit.

Now would be a good time to mention my roller balls. The wheels on my suitcase were the old-fashioned kind: under-sized and prone to jamming. They were working in such a limp, tired manner, and my things were packed so top-heavy, that my suitcase kept falling over. I wanted it to glide dutifully behind me wherever I went. Instead, I kept having to pick it up off the floor, right it, and try again.

So I slogged my suitcase and leather backpack to the most reasonable place I could think of: the bar. I dragged myself and all my crap through the bar, twice, over the thick carpet, trying to decide where to sit, where to go, what to do.

I picked a seat up at the bar, on the end, with room for my massive, green and pink, designer, upholstered luggage, my backpack and me. I ordered a glass of red wine and was halfway through it before I noticed two men smoking and talking next to me. (Everyone in Egypt smokes Marlboro Reds—for the heartiest of smokers, Marlboro Lights in the white box, Merits occasionally, and the crappy local brand, Cleopatra.) I tapped the young man sitting closest to me on the shoulder. "Excuse me. I'm having the worst day of my life. Can I have one of your cigarettes, please?"

Enter Prince Charming and Prince Charminger.

The two men turned around. "Sure," said the man, Patrick, sitting next to my neighbor. He pulled a Marlboro Light from his pack.

The next most obvious question came: "So why is this the worst day..?"

Out came the story. At least the best of the worst of it.

Patrick, a communications manager with Hyatt Hotels, lit my cigarette. Hailing from Holland, he was tall, slender, and utterly professional in that totally hip, young, successful way. I recognized part of myself in him, when I was 27 and on the rise in a mega-corporation: smart, capable, and with my whole, great, grownup life ahead of me.

Patrick instantly got on his cell phone and started calling around downtown Cairo for a room somewhere for me. The man next to me, meanwhile, James from South Africa, listened to me ramble on about the minutia of my novel and my research trip to Egypt. His genuine interest seemed like a good omen to me—that this adventure was real and right and good—and for the first time in a long time, I started feeling better.

I bought Patrick and James both a beer and we started swapping travel stories. The conversation went on for over an hour, then another hour. Hotel bars are dark and transient ports of call, witnesses to endless comings and goings and happenings in between. I think of them as human waypoints and I love them.

I didn't even notice, until James pointed it out later, that I was the only woman in the whole bar. Neither did it occur to me that not that long ago, women weren't even *allowed* in bars in Egypt. I had also forgotten the hunger and the weariness that brought me there. The princes and I were enjoying that happy, intense and temporary friendship that only passing travelers know. And for two blessed hours, I felt as though I wasn't alone in a great, big, weird, heartless country.

"More wine, please." Big tip, peanuts for dinner. "Would you like another cigarette?" "Yes, thank you." Tarak, the bartender, served up a dish of cucumbers, olives and carrots. I passed on those, told never to eat fruit or vegetables in Egypt that I hadn't washed and peeled myself. Like the stupid Canadian Rule, the stupid Vegetable Rule was destined for the mental landfill.

As my prospects for a room that night dimmed with each return call to Patrick, James offered to share his room with me. "Really, if you'd like," he said shyly, knowing he just delivered the great pick-up line of the modern era, or at least of this trip. I didn't see one trace of expectation or cupidity in his face. "Even if you would just like to take my key, and shower, and sleep for awhile."

In that moment, I knew I would be safe on that first dark night in Cairo. I said only, "Maybe. Thank you very much. Maybe."

They fascinated me, these young world travelers of commerce and conversation. James, a consultant to the Egyptian textile industry, stayed at the Hilton regularly and they treated him like the respectable, well-heeled customer he was. So he went to Reception to try to extend his reservation for a few days on my behalf. Though he would leave for Luxor the next morning, he tried to guarantee his room for me, for 68 dollars a night—a Thank You God good price.

Regardless, the hotel said no. Every room was spoken for.

Stranded, bewildered, running on red wine and adrenaline alone, I accepted James' offer for the night. We bade hearty and warm goodbyes to Patrick and stumbled to James' room like two sophomore coeds on a bender. I showered, grateful more than ever for hot running water, took a swig of Pepto-Bismol for good measure, and brushed my teeth in the sink. *Don't drink the tap water.* This was the third Rule I broke in Egypt.

James signed me onto Hotmail on his laptop, connected through his cell phone. How perfect was that? I needed to rescind my *Urgent From Cairo* five-alarm emails smoldering on the Internet. "I'm saying the nicest things about you," I said to James, as I penned my emails to America.

"Really?" He wanted to know what I had written, so I read it back to him. I don't remember exactly what I said. Something about two compassionate heroes, and being in a hotel room with a blonde Dennis Quaid who spoke with a charming accent.

From the couch and the bed, James and I talked until after three in the morning, turning the light on once to smoke cigarettes. We discussed politics and apartheid, advertising and prejudice, things we are taught from childhood, and the freedoms of speech, religion and enterprise. We talked about his wife and three children, and why I'm afraid of the dark. We talked about his trip to Luxor and how maybe we could meet up again there.

We finally admitted that we needed rest. James promised not to cuddle up in the night even though he was bunking with a "beautiful American woman." He overstated the compliment vastly, but in Egypt, blessings whispered in the night have magic in them. I would not argue the point. James kept his promise, and eventually, silently ensconced on our respective sides of the room, we slept.

My eyes snapped open three hours later, wide awake from vivid dreams and worry. One hour until 7 A.M. and James' wake-up call. I padded to the bathroom, reminding myself who and where I was, and why. I had Medusa hair. I had inadequate rest, a red wine hangover, a strange man across the room, and a hotel problem.

I slunk back to the couch. The city came alive with the incessant beeping of car horns, unruly traffic and voices from the street. Outside the hotel window, beyond the balcony and the rooftop terrace, Cairo drew itself out in a lavender pink haze. Did a morning ever break to find me more befuddled?

I dared to watch James for awhile, still sleeping sweetly. I stood there wishing I had perfect, bone-straight, blunt-cut, swishy hair. The kind of hair that looks good in the mornings even if you sleep on it wet. It struck me as beyond ridiculous to be worried about bad hair when I had epic problems resting on my shoulders that day. But here's the truth that only curly-haired people know: things just *go* better when your hair looks good.

On paper, spending one's first night in a foreign country with a strange man in el Nil Hilton seems well beyond the limits of propriety. And outrageously, stupendously crazy.

Fine. But as it turned out—except for the hair—it was perfect. It turned out that men played a great role in my Egyptian adventures. I made friends with zero Egyptian women; in fact, I never even met any in person.

I've woven the names of these men and their stories into these pages, because they wrote the story of Egypt for me as clearly and concisely as the land and the legends of travel books. More so. Most of the men I encountered were kind, sincere, warmhearted and friendly guys, who I liked very much. A few were not. Take the Israeli businessman, for example, who suggested I keep him company in his room during the long layover in Greece on the way to Cairo. Or we could go to *my* room, if I preferred. That suggestion didn't play out so well for him. A self-proclaimed "rich Lebanese playboy" introduced himself to me at the Hilton bar one night. That didn't go where he hoped it would, either. A few random men who passed by me on the busy Cairo streets hissed angrily in my face, but I was more surprised than threatened. I thought one guy on a bus had plans to kill me, but more on that later.

Why so many men? Why so many intimate, innocent encounters with strangers from the opposite sex? Aside from the plain fact that I ran across something like 100:1 more men than women in Egypt, I have no idea. I'm not a man magnet. If I sat alone in a bar in Seattle or Los Angeles or Bend, I would totally be ignored. I know this because, as a frequent traveler, I've passed a great many hours, layovers, and solo meals in cocktail lounges.

Nor am I am great maker of friends. I'm naturally shy, and because I have a weird name, I've always been uncomfortable introducing myself to people. My friendships are few and deep and hard earned. Sheltered, shy and confused from the start, I learned about life from music and books. When I was about nine years old, I got my first library card and right about that same time, I decided two important things about my life:

1. I would read every book in the library. I didn't realize that the beautiful collection on those shelves—with their alluring combination of knowledge and fantasy—were not finite in number. I didn't know that new books rolled off the press every day; that the library was a living thing, never to be wholly consumed.

2. I also decided that I would be like Nancy Drew, or Rebecca of Sunnybrook Farm—the sort of person who knew everyone in town and enjoyed love, admiration and respect. A stint on a local city council with a Smart Growth agenda will send that notion racing quickly down the toilet. In my case, I was venerated by few, unloved by many—to say it delicately—and flat-out vilified in the local paper. I can assure you, neither Nancy nor Rebecca ever held public office.

While my childhood fantasies bended to the laws of reality, one unexpected theme emerged in my life: I loved men. I cherished them. I'm not the most popular girl on the block, or stunningly attractive, but I can make pals with most men in a heartbeat. Perhaps because I grew up tomboy-ish, adoring my older brother, Ken, and younger cousin, Sam. I followed them up and down the banks of Ashby Creek in Montana, hiking, fishing, shooting, and doing whatever else they dared to do. If Ken climbed the giant cottonwood tree to peer into the nest of sky-blue robin's eggs, then so would I. If Sam put a firecracker in a cow pie and then lit it, well, it was my turn next.

As much fun as I had in my youth, however, I could never translate that into longterm, romantic relationships. One year max, and my work there was done. Until I met Mike, I'd driven away as many men as I'd left behind. There wasn't a person, a place or a thing that I couldn't leave behind. The inheritance of an abandoned childhood, I suppose. This is not to say that certain relationships, when they ended, didn't bring me to my knees. They did. Pat, for example, of the dreamy sea-green eyes, and the rabid streak of jealousy. Clark, beautiful Clark, moody writer and best kisser of all time.

I love them still, in that sweet, sorry way that memories cost; memories that won't die. To this day, I still admire men. I love the way they smell: all spicy and sweaty and warm. I love the way their hair looks in the morning: rumpled and slept-in and perfect. I love the crap men say: how they can cuss like dockworkers and still sound dignified. I love the way they have muscles: that they can lift things that I can't, open jars, dip me on the dance floor. I love their tenderness, and the vulnerability they hide behind the sports talk. I love how they can be moody and self-contained, in ways I can never be. I love it that they're mostly tall. I love tuxedos and starched, pink dress shirts with silk ties. I love thick, faded red cotton T-shirts and blue jeans. I love that place on the body of a man where his shoulder meets his neck: that warm, soft nook that perfectly fits a woman's cheek.

I. Love. Men. And I'm so curious about them. I want to know them, to peel back the mystery that surrounds them and separates their outward selves from the secrets inside. Maybe that's why it was easy to make friends in Egypt. Curiosity drew us toward each other. Or maybe we inhabit a lonely world, and we search out ways to fill pockets of emptiness. We want something to hold onto, albeit temporarily. A mirror perhaps, to remind us who we are, to tell us that we are not alone.

Half an hour until James' wake-up call. I lay there, thinking. Ten minutes more, two minutes. The television blasted on at 7:01 A.M. to rugby championships. James flew to the remote control. I expected a kinder, gentler wake-up call—a woman on the phone, perhaps, whispering good morning with a dreamy accent. No. I was on an adventure of a different sort, where wake-up calls come blaring in Arabic over the television set.

I sat up and tried to smooth down my hair. Why hadn't I just taken a shower when I first woke up? Nipped the hair problem in the bud?

James and I smoked cigarettes and chatted shyly on the balcony before he left. We talked about meeting up in Luxor in a few days. I had this crazy notion that we actually might do it. We would stay at the Winter Palace Hotel, with its Victorian façade and isolated gardens. James would work all day and I would explore the monuments, and we'd come together at night. We would drink wine at street cafes in the dusky evening light, as people passed us by. We'd eat exotic food and experiment with new tastes and we'd share our tales of the day.

But no. I had a sort-of boyfriend and James had a wife and I was alone on this journey. I hugged James good-bye. One moment just looking at each other, then he closed the door behind him.

CHAPTER TWO

FIRST DAZE: UNIMAGINABLE CHAOS

KHEPERA: *Khepera, the rising sun, is regarded as self-created and is depicted as a scarab beetle. He is the symbol of daily resurrection. From ancient Egypt to the Roman Empire, beetle amulets were worn to invoke the power and protection of the god, Khepera, and the notion of rebirth in the new day.*

My first morning in Cairo startled the hell out of me. Traffic works in an unimaginable state of chaos. Add to that, pedestrians are everywhere. Like an unstrung orchestra in an insane asylum, the cars and people move in a symphony of beeping horns and darting bodies. In America, we have a system: green for go, red for stop, and yellow for no guts, no glory. That would seem unbelievably *ridiculous* to the Cairenes, and a colossal waste of time. Their system goes like this: *I'll move through you if you don't hit me. I won't hit you if you get your ass out of my way.* It's as simple and as mind-boggling as that. In Cairo, they're all about the guts and the glory.

The sidewalks are for selling; the streets are for walking. Cutting in and around and out, the people move through the moving cars, sometimes very nearly touching them. It is *unreal*, and I was certain my cab driver was going to hit more than one pedestrian, more than once. *Beep-beep, coming through*, the horns never stop. Drivers totally ignore the marked lanes and stoplights, though at some random intersections a traffic cop occasionally holds out a candy-cane-colored baton and whistles traffic into a loose, temporary obedience. Somehow this crazy, lunatic system works—for the hearty and the young, and for the little old ladies covered head-to-toe in their black *chadors*, crossing six lanes of fast moving, maniacal traffic. It's a dance, of sorts: a dangerous fast-paced haphazard line dance.

I never figured out if this system let every man, woman and child fend for himself, or if it inspired a hard-driven respect for the unknown individual—within the context of getting oneself to where one is going.

Through all this, a man rides his bike. On his head—*his head*—he carries a 10-foot-long pallet, stacked with loaves upon loaves of loose pita bread, piled two-feet high. This is the absolute truth. He holds the pallet with one hand and steers his bike through the mayhem with the other. *Ching-ching*, he chimes a bell on his handlebars, *coming through*.

On James' advice, in case the Hilton didn't work out—which of course it didn't—I checked into the Grand Hotel. Located on a very busy downtown street, the Grand Hotel is old, rustic, and endlessly charming. More so, if I wasn't the one and only Caucasian staying in the entire building. Or if it wasn't *quite* so old, or *quite* so noisy. Still, I adored the white marble staircase worn soft through the decades. Though it unnerved me to ride it, I liked the tired, old lift, with its two sets of doors—the outer of swinging glass, the inner of sliding metal—which barely had room for both my suitcase and me. I liked that room number 101 had a big balcony that looked out over the street to an open-air bazaar. I liked the Persian carpets on the hardwood floors, and the tiled bathroom—bigger than my bedroom back home.

I did not like the armed guard outside. Or those posted on all the adjacent streets, for that matter. Tourist police were everywhere in Egypt, and even after seeing so many of them over the weeks, I never got used to them. Bored men, like the one outside the Grand Hotel—young and armed with automatic rifles—smoked cigarettes and killed time on every street in downtown Cairo and at all the tombs and temples, monuments and museums. Stationed there to protect travelers like me, they also served a constant reminder that I needed protecting.

But I didn't come to Cairo to cower in my hotel room. So I took one, small, determined step at a time—always figuring out how, where, how much, how long. Then mustering my courage to step out. By noon the first day I had made every possible mistake: overpaying taxis, drinking tap water, losing my hotel confirmation. I felt great.

I got blithely, ignorantly over-charged for my cab ride to the Grand Hotel and back to the Hilton for lunch. My pirate cab driver, Mosen Eid (he spelled his name carefully for me so I could find him whenever I needed) assured me over and over that he would "be right with me." His logic was that if he cheated me, I wouldn't use him again. He was right. What I couldn't understand was why he assumed I wouldn't discover that 50 pounds was too much money for a round trip of five blocks one way and five blocks back. The next time I would see Mosen Eid, two weeks later and quite by chance, a fight would break out over me between him and another cab driver. In the meantime, I figured out how to negotiate the maze between the two hotels on foot.

Of the many mistakes I made, the first one involved the packing of a curling iron. I am one of life's obsessive people who use a curling iron every day to straighten my hair. Straight-haired people can never figure this out. But curly-haired people, we *know*. None-the-less, my wide-tube, Revlon Pro, curling/straightening device was useless. Cairo has a strain of humidity, and humidity is the great deal-breaker in this backwards coiffing system. Besides that, the voltage didn't direct enough current through the adapter to heat my curling iron properly. That settled it: I'd go curly though Egypt.

Lunching alone in a foreign country is a wonderful thing. I could order anything I wanted, study my guidebooks, make notes in my journal, and watch an exotic world unfold around me.

My first Cairo lunch took place on a warm café terrace at the Hilton. I ordered a club sandwich, red wine and Marlboro in the white pack. I got white wine and Marlboro reds. The wine I drank; the cigarettes I returned. The sandwich, surprisingly like the ones at Denny's, came later.

The terrace overlooked a peaceful Tahrir Square, with a grassy gathering place to the right, and the Egyptian Museum to the left. Two years prior, in front of that same museum, three men sprayed automatic weapon fire into a crowd of tourists. Nine people died on the pavement that day, and another 19 were injured before policemen and onlookers brought the terrorists down.

Tahrir Square, which translates in English to *Liberation Square*, has long played a dramatic role in modern Egyptian culture and politics. Eighty years before I had a club sandwich in Tahrir Square, Egypt and Sudan rose up against British rule in the Egyptian Revolution of 1919. One brave and inspired woman, Hoda Shaarawi, cast off her veil here, in full public view. While the action caused the religious establishment to soil their pants, and it was too shocking at the time for broad appeal, Hoda continued through her life to fight for women's rights to divorce and the abolition of polygamy.

After the 23 July Revolution in 1952, a military coup that changed Egypt from a constitutional monarchy into a republic, this popular gathering place was officially changed from Ismailia Square to Tahrir Square.

Over 300,000 people came to Tahrir Square in January/February 2011 in the 18 Day Egyptian Revolution, rallying to oust corrupt president, Hosni Mubarak. Violent clashes between security forces and protesters killed 846 people and injured another 6,000 before Mubarak resigned from the office he held for nearly 30 years, on February 11.

I walked past a billboard on a busy street in Cairo, right outside of a McDonalds, ironically, with a portrait of Mubarak wearing the green crown of America's Statue of Liberty. It was not a comforting image. All these years later, the fallen president will stand trial for abusing power, the pre-meditated murder of peaceful protesters, and collusion in the assassination of his predecessor, Anwar Sadat. Meanwhile all the businessmen who thrived during Mubarak's tenure are getting nervous, as the Supreme Council of the Armed Forces turns its angry gaze on those who prospered through the ex-president's good graces.

Today, this epicenter of Egyptian culture holds its secrets and its promises, its moments of despair and hope, within the threads of daily life.

"You have beautiful eyes."

The policeman at the Egyptian Museum wore his machine gun casually, as if it were no more threatening than an umbrella, as if flirting with a tourist while wearing a badge and an automatic weapon wasn't odd in the slightest. It made me wonder how seriously he took his job. It made me wonder, what, if anything, he could do about a cadre of angry terrorists.

"Thank you," I mumbled. It was my habit to ignore comments from passing men in Egypt. But I liked to imagine that I *did* have Egyptian eyes, olive in shape and color, and lined with pencil. Mysterious, exotic. But I don't. Egyptian eyes are brown.

You must pay extra to take a camera into the Egyptian Museum, which I found out once I was at the entrance. They promptly sent me back to the ticket booth. *Another 5 pounds please.* Fine. I couldn't actually *use* said camera, of course. I carried a little instamatic camera that day, with auto-everything: auto-load, auto-advance, auto-rewind, auto-flash. Idiot-proof. No flash photography in the museum, however. Great. I'd paid extra for a camera I couldn't use.

No flash photography. That was the rule. Now, my grandmother had raised me to be a rule-follower and a rule-follower I was. So, while prowling the long, dusty halls of the museum, I couldn't help but notice a certain Asian couple. Moving from statue to statue, they snapped flash after flash of each other, posed obliviously in front of the artifacts, grinning with great satisfaction. Artifacts that were, say, oh, 6,000 years old and sensitive to light, as an example. Why did they think the rules didn't apply to them? I briefly entertained the notion of snatching the camera out of their hands and personally escorting them to a certain machine gun toting policeman I knew. Millions of tourists visit the Egyptian Museum each year and none are allowed to take flash photography. Except these two? My grandmother would have a thing or two to say about that.

People moved through the crowded halls in hot, lingering clusters; noisy shuffling throngs following their tour guides from one exhibit to the next. I strolled through slowly, letting the various collections wash over me and sink under my skin. It astonished me to gaze at the remnants of other people's lives, people who lived and breathed and loved, here, hundreds and thousands of years ago. Colossal statues mingled with pottery, everyday household items, jewelry, coffins, figurines, busts, tools and alabaster jars: artifacts of kings and paupers long dead.

The Egyptian Museum houses over 120,000 artifacts, from ancient history to the Greco-Roman period. This includes the golden throne of Tutankaman—not your average run-of-the-mill chair. The legs are detailed as those of a lion, and the arm panels take the shape of winged cobras. This throne, covered in silver and gold and inlaid with semiprecious jewels, held the weight of a king 3,300 years ago. Being a pharaoh had its privileges; being a god incarnate was another thing altogether.

What also fascinated me was what *was not* in the museum. The bust of Queen Nefertiti, for example. Nefertiti means *the beauty that has come* and if her likeness is to be believed, it's absolutely true. One of the most famous artifacts from ancient Egypt depicts this beautiful queen—a stunning likeness, carved and painted and abandoned for 3,257 years in a sculptor's workshop.

But Nefertiti's famous image doesn't reside among the relics in the Egyptian Museum. No. You'll find Nefertiti in Berlin, at the Altes Museum. Which seemed odd to me. If she *must* be an ambassador of Egyptian tourism, couldn't this most beautiful of queens be at the Louvre, instead? At least she'd be under the same roof as the crown jewels of France and the Venus de Milo. Nefertiti would most certainly appreciate fine wine and beautiful clothes, and she might even enjoy a media junket in the City of Lights. Instead, her spirit roams the Altes at night, drinking thick beer and discussing philosophy with Nietzsche. Perhaps she is happy there. But I think not. I think she's haunting the dark corridors, wafting down the halls to the darkened windows, trying to get home.

Lost in thoughts of Nefertiti's plight, I rounded a corner, only to be confronted by her husband: Akhenaton. Akhenaton, known as the heretic pharaoh of the New Kingdom (circa 1,350 b.c.), married the beautiful daughter of a soldier and forged a revolution with her at his side. I had studied countless photographs of Akhenaton's image in books and films. Now here he was, immortalized, in front of me. I wanted to reach out and touch him, to say, *Hello, it's me, Kyla. I know you. I came here to see you.* I just looked up and stared. Akhenaton lays claim to great intrigue and speculation. Aside from being the most radical of the Egyptian kings, he was also the most odd-looking. Statues, wall reliefs and papyri all render him as tall and soft, with a protruding belly, over-sized lips, and a long, narrow face. Magnificent.

Akhenaton rejected the pantheon of gods that Egyptians had worshipped for centuries, and around which elaborate rituals and offerings had been constructed. Instead, Akhenaton favored only one god: Ra, the Sun god, the source of all life. In a shocking and unprecedented upheaval, Akhenaton moved the capitol city from Luxor to Armana, where he built his shining new kingdom in the sun.

This outlandish pharaoh is thought to have been the father of young Tutankhamun. While Akhenaton had many followers, most of the Egyptian people simply could not accept his radical, sweeping changes, and he was thought to have met a violent and untimely end. Upon his death, Tutankhamun took the throne and, under the supervision of the marginalized priests of old, the much-loved boy King restored Egypt to its former traditions. Still, Akhenaton remains one of the most enigmatic and compelling characters in Egyptian history, advocating monotheism a millennium before modern religion did the same.

I stayed and stayed, transfixed by every detail of Akhenaton's statue, and came back again to stay some more. Busy enclaves continued to move through the museum in pushy little clumps, stopping and starting and stopping again. I did everything in my power to avoid them. Until my final destination.

I made my way to the funerary cache of the famous King Tut, housed in a special room, dimly lit and subject to a constant stream of curious travelers. I joined the milieu, eager to see the fabled treasures. The vast and splendid artifacts, intended to accompany Tutankhamun through the afterlife, were dug out of a hole in the ground in 1923 by archaeologist Howard Carter. From a lost and forgotten tomb in the Valley of the Kings came the *piece d'resistance*: Tut's death mask. Made of gold and lapis, so rare and so stunning, it has commanded the world's attention since its discovery. And there it was: the solid gold replica of the face of a king, staring back at me across the centuries. This boy, this god, who died too young and was hidden in the sand. I stood there and cried.

Walking back to my hotel, a little lost, I nearly walked into a moving car. I never figured out, the whole time, how people knew which cars would stop for you and which ones would not. A young man helped me through the traffic and walked along with me, very fast, speaking all the while. He was a teacher at the American University in Cairo.

Where are you from? Where are you staying? Is this your first time in Egypt? I would be asked these same questions over and over during my visit.

"You must stay at the student hostel," Speedy Man insisted. "Five pounds a night. It's just over there... you understand? I can show you."

"Oh, thank you, I'll just stay at my hotel."

"You must say *shokran*. Not, 'thank you.' Say *shokran*."

"Oh, *shokran*," I repeated, "*Shokran, shokran*."

"*Afwan*," he replied. Then he talked about an IZ card—and though I never really learned what it was—my new teacher promised it would save me 50% on everything. "You understand?" And he could show me where to get one. "You understand?"

"Yes. *Shokran, shokran*." Whatever. He was walking way too fast. And talking way too much. You understand?

"I am going to have coffee," he announced. "Would you like to come?"

He was really very nice, and harmless I suspect, just a sprinkle high strung. "No, thank you. *Shokran*. I am going to my hotel."

"I will walk you there."

"*Shokran*."

"*Afwan. Afwan*." Nothing, don't mention it.

"Can you have coffee now?"

"No, I just want to go to my hotel."

"What for?"

"To rest."

"Maybe we could have coffee later?"

"No. Thank you. *Shokran*. Thank you very much for your help. I have to say good-bye now. *Shokran*."

"*Afwan*," he waved his hand. We walked in opposite directions.

That afternoon I mustered the courage to take the good camera out onto the streets. This was the borrowed camera, the expensive, 35mm camera. The camera that I was still learning how to use. But it wasn't the camera I was afraid of. It was leaving my hotel room.

During a bout of fear before I left America, one of my friends said that if all I ever did for two weeks in Egypt was sit in my hotel room, my trip would still be an incredible thing. *Riiight*.

So I strapped on my camera and my courage and set out amongst the crowds. My first stop was the open-air bazaar right across the street, which was not very far to venture my first time out for some serious picture taking. Some photographers may feel invisible behind their cameras, protected, once-removed. The camera makes them official. (Who else could stand up at the front of a wedding ceremony or a Christmas pageant when everyone else is respectfully seated? Who else gets to haunt the sidelines of the Super Bowl field besides coaches and players? Only photographers.)

In my case, my camera made me conspicuous. As if I wasn't strange looking enough already. This was a small local bazaar, not part of the tourist route, crowded with people conducting the serious business of their daily lives. And here I was, odd-man-out, taking pictures of produce.

By now I'm really wishing I *was* invisible. I wanted to be able to move slowly and take pictures of people who didn't know they were being observed. So I started snapping the shutter at *things*—storefronts, buildings, chickens, stacks of eggs. Eventually, I got the courage to ask, "Can I take your picture?" *Click-click*, I imitated with my finger. Most people were nice about the whole thing, though some must have thought I was insane. I tried to imagine their dinner conversations: *So, how was the market? Fine, fine, fresh eggs; I found a new fry pan that I like. Some white woman took a picture of my pomegranates, though. Weird.*

One man put his arm proudly around his banana display and beamed his toothless grin my way. I admire a man who's confident in his produce. And his smile. One very shy young girl acquiesced to my request and smiled into my lens, although she hid behind, but only half-behind, her big sister.

Even the scary tourist cop by my hotel accommodated a photo, although he didn't know it. Something I just *knew* never to do was to walk up to a policeman and take his headshot. So I took a picture of the necktie shop next door, and I just happened to make sure he was in the narrow right-hand margin of the frame.

This might be a good time to mention merchandising. In Cairo, window displays are not like what you see at Neiman Marcus—all staged and sexy. No. In Cairo, shopkeepers cram at least one of every single item for sale into their window displays. So a necktie shop will have, say, 100 neckties dangling in the window. A shoe store: fifty pairs. Clothing: a closet full. Pots and pans: don't even try to count. It gives you a feeling of abundance, though. If you see it, you can buy it. If you need it, they have it. And then some. Their cups runneth over.

Skipping back to my hotel room, with a full roll of film in hand, I felt abundant, too—as fancy and overflowing as a window full of shoes.

CHAPTER THREE
GIFTS: LOST AND FOUND

APOPHIS: *Apophis is the snake god, the god of darkness, enemy of the sun-god Ra. It is Apophis' blood that stains the skies each morning and evening as the struggle between light and dark endlessly repeats itself.*

I had checked into the Grand Hotel as a stopgap, a temporary fix. After the Hilton fiasco, however, I needed a Plan B. My guidebook said that there was an amazing, reasonably priced hotel in Garden City. After one night, I said goodbye to the Grand, hauled my luggage to the curb, grabbed a cab, and headed toward the Garden City House—where I would spend my next few days in a kinder, gentler, area of Cairo. Garden City, after all, is graced by world embassies and expensive shopping. The guidebook promised "breakfast conversations with resident archaeologists and scholars" and a view of the Nile. How could I go wrong?

Wednesday / November 10 / Cairo

My cab driver got lost. Totally, irrevocably lost. Here's the thing about cabbies: You ask, *Do you know how to find the Garden City House?* Answer: *Yes, yes, come this way. Here, I'll take your luggage.* So my driver promptly takes me to the Shepheard's Hotel. On his behalf, I will admit that the Shepheard's is *in* Garden City. It's nice, expensive, five stars, famous, built in the 19 century, occupied by the British in World War II, luxuriously renovated, and exactly *not* the right place for me.

So off we go again. I mean, I *have the address* in my guidebook. And the exact name of the hotel. I have a telephone number and a three star rating. This time we get really lost. We end up on a dead end road, packed with pedestrians. Six Arab men surround the car and the cab driver is asking them directions and they're all pointing this way and that, shouting instructions, arguing with each other. Bear in mind, I've checked out of my hotel. I have nowhere to go.

After an hour of general confusion, high heat and mounting stress, we park across the street from the Garden City House. It looked like a Warsaw ghetto, or remnants of a gang war: stark, cement blocks behind a chain link fence on a major thoroughfare, surrounded by more sad buildings of stark, cement blocks. But there it is, painted on the outside wall: Garden City House. "How about we go back to the Grand Hotel?" suggests the cabdriver. I am so all over that. "Yes, yes, please." We were so obviously in the wrong place and I was melting hot, wired for sound, and happy to throw Plan B to the wolves.

Then we get lost, again. We couldn't find our way to the Grand Hotel, where we started. That put me back at the great hub of tourist activity, with my heavy suitcase in tow: The Nile Hilton.

Next I met Amr.

Amr was a gift I never asked for and never dreamed of and can't imagine what I would have done without. He was determined to take me under his wing and make sure I was safe and happy in Egypt. And he was wildly capable in his abilities. Add to this, he was intelligent—in facts and abstraction, philosophy and spirit. His heart seemed too big for a world populated with people obsessed with themselves. Like, oh, I don't know, say, *me* for example.

But I didn't know all this yet.

We would spend a lot of time together in the following weeks, talking. We didn't talk of the weather or fashion or sports. We talked of politics, religion, foreign cultures, mentors, fear, hate, terror, loss, and love.

Here was a successful, busy, international business owner, burdened with a thousand details, on the run every day, a family both older and younger to care for, friends, colleagues, employees, and business associates all in constant orbit around him. And here was a man who carved out time for me, every day, arranged a thousand impossible details on my behalf, and had the grace to miss me when I was gone.

Amr was late. I waited in the Hilton's lobby writing in my journal, smoking Marlboro Lights. I forgave him for being late, nearly immediately, for his unexpected and almost incomprehensible generosity of spirit. Amr would later take my pen and write things in that same journal. He wrote in English for me, and backwards in Arabic for the taxi drivers who would deliver me into the heart of the city. He would also write down the appropriate cab fare. So I knew. So they knew I knew.

That first evening, over dinner, Amr pulled an American dollar from his wallet— a bill soft and old and worn. One dollar bill with a story to tell:

Amr had been sent by his father to England to study when he was only 17. He spoke no English when he landed in London, and spent most of his time being alone, sad and confused. He didn't understand the words, concepts or instructions people said to him, and he had no friends.

One day his American professor-in-residence posed a complicated equation to his students, with the reward of one dollar to whoever could solve it first. The European crowd declined. Amr stood up to the chalkboard and slowly, calmly solved the problem. It was a physics professor, as I recall, and a question of failure points.

Amr has carried that worn fold of legal tender in his wallet for 25 years. He carries it still.

He gave me the bill to hold as he related the story. I can still feel the paper in my fingers, the satin texture, the faded colors, the folds and wrinkles. These are the sensations that remind me of courage and tenacity. They remind me that nothing is impossible. They remind me of Amr. They also make me imagine quantum failure points, and all these neutrons and electrons bumping into each other saying, *Don't let me down. I rely on you. Without you, this system fails.*

Amr treated me to a comprehensive taste of Egypt that night, at the Semiramis Intercontinental Hotel— his favorite restaurant and the most luxurious hotel in Cairo. He said he goes there whenever the world gets too noisy. He goes there all by himself, just to forget it all, and hear the sounds of silence.

Shall we begin with soup?

The food was laid out in a sumptuous buffet. I followed Amr like a loyal duckling as he filled plates for me. Soup, appetizers, salads, entrées. He described each of 50 choices, and served up those I chose, passed by those I didn't. Occasionally he would insist that I *try just a little, eat only what you like.*

"This one is spicy, you won't want that."

"Oh, yes I do, please."

An hour into our culinary affair, we paused for a cigarette break. We talked on and on. Then we ate some more. "Now let me seduce you into Egyptian desserts," he said.

My eyes grew the size of salad plates. "Oh no. Really, I'm full. Really, thanks."

"I will fix a little plate for you. Eat only what you like." Amr left the table and carefully selected a little plate of this and that. He apologized when he came back. "I didn't mean to *seduce* you. I saw your eyes..."

"I know. You meant to *lure* me."

"Yes, that's it. To lure you."

At this point I would have started all over at the beginning, just not to disappoint him. I was terribly overfed. Warmed from the insides.

Finally Amr walked me through the hotel, showing me all the other restaurants and the casino. Then he saw my face and dropped me back at my hotel. I was still so very tired.

Amr met me again the next day. The Nile Hilton was becoming my launching pad. It was the place every taxi driver knew how to get to, and the place where I could check my email, to link myself with home through anxious friends. It was where I exchanged money, made phone calls, met Amr, and stopped in at evening time, after each long day, to drink red wine, talk with Tarak the bartender, and write in my journal.

Amr was late again. We took a taxi ride to the heart of the business district. Amr had this wacky idea that I needed a *plan.* I thought that I could just show up in Egypt, find a train to all the remote places I wanted to see, and secure a hotel room whenever I got there.

"It doesn't work that way," Amr explained. Definitely not in high season. And even if I could, it wasn't safe.

Amr convinced me to do what I had rejected from the beginning: take a tour on what I considered the Love Boat of the Nile—a cruise ship. I didn't want my trip to be sterile, squeaky clean, common. I wanted to explore the nether-regions. I wanted to see the *real* Egypt.

But I was increasingly worried about money. If I learned one thing in Egypt, it was this: whatever troublesome issues I have in life, and whatever natural gifts, they will be exponentially magnified on a trip like this. Thus, I made terrific acquaintances and I freaked out about money. I hadn't saved enough. I was going to run out in a week.

Four nights on *The Nile Romance* was $660. This included full board, a flight from Cairo to Luxor, a cruise south to Aswan, guided trips every day, and a flight back from Aswan to Cairo. (Did I mention I hate to fly?) Still Amr insisted, "It will be the highlight of your trip to Egypt. You can lay by the pool (in my non-existent bikini), eat yourself sick, and see all the great monuments."

The highlight of my trip to Egypt would be the people, but Amr was making a strong point: I could only get upstream—to the many amazing and ancient monuments—by boat.

$660 was a very good price. *Monsieur* Dorrey, Amr's travel agent, made it happen—for Amr, his very good customer—when everything in Egypt was over-booked. One woman at another agency said to Amr, "Luxor? You must be joking!" Amr translated it for me after we left her office. We went to two travel agencies so Amr could verify the good price we'd been offered from *Monsieur* Dorrey. Which tells you something about him.

"I'll think about it," I said, still worried about money, and fighting the idea that I couldn't just catch a train south. I wanted to see al-Qsar, for example, a village in my novel, where the discoverers of the Gnostic Gospels had lived. James had told me already, though, that to go to that region required an armed caravan.

Instead of the cruise, I wanted to fly to Luxor ($125), and meet James for two days. He would work and I would explore. I would visit the Winter Palace Hotel (former residence of King Farouk), the Luxor Museum, and the Temple of Hatchepsut. I would explore these in detail—all these settings in my novel. I would take pictures. James and I would drink wine and eat cheese on a patio overlooking the Nile. We would talk until late into the night, past the time we were tired. We would laugh, and as in Cairo, practice American and British accents on each other. We would learn.

Then I would say good-bye forever and take a bus to the south coast of Sinai, then a boat across the Red Sea. A short trek by car would take me to the monastery of St. Catherine's. There I would walk the land of Moses, hear the pilgrims chant, and touch the face of God.

It was a complicated, exquisite plan, relying on my ingenuity and skills as a seasoned world traveler and rugged individualist. Forget the fact that I'm about as rugged and seasoned as a croissant. I secretly knew it wouldn't happen as I imagined. Because even my cab drivers got lost.

Thursday / November 11 / Veterans Day / Cairo

I finally had the severe meltdown that had been brewing for days. I drank too much wine the night before and woke up with no bottled water. I was hung over and homesick and drank from the sink. I wanted biscuits and gravy at the Snow Bunny Café. I wanted a cup of herbal tea, and transactions in American dollars. I wanted the company of the familiar.

I was nearly halfway across the globe, and I didn't have enough money. I woke up at 4:30 in the morning, sat up in bed, and cried for having misplanned my trip, for being lonesome, homesick, and still half afraid.

There was nothing else to do: I was going to have to borrow some money from my dad. My father was generous with me throughout my life. But it was embarrassing to have to ask, to be a grown woman calling on the International Bank of Daddy-O.

When I was in school my father gave me a dollar bill for every 'A' I brought home on my report card. Then he added a bi-weekly allowance. Then he paid for my college education. He had demonstrated his support time and again, and I was feeling like a miserable failure. I wasn't on the same path as my brother who, like all the accomplished people, owned a house by now, married and had settled into a life of security.

My dad was a college track star in 1956, with Olympic prospects. He was farmraised in Eastern Montana, strong and lean and fast. He broke distance records like eggshells and collected metals like my generation collected Hot Wheels. Then he met my mom, and Ken was born, and that was the end of that. He was 19. I came 14 months later. Two days prior to my noisy arrival, he turned 21.

I was two months old when he left his wife and babies to join the army. He came back for a short stint—I'm told, though I don't remember it—to work in the saw mill. It must have been a keen instinct for self-preservation that took him to Seattle to get a desk job.

My mom, 19 and out of her depth, held onto Ken for another year, but I was promptly given to the care of my aunt and uncle. That lasted about another two months before they issued their own ultimatum: We adopt her and make her our own, or no deal. They had the foresight to see what would eventually come, when regret or longing made my parents change their minds.

No deal. No adoption. So I was sent to live with my grandparents, who had fewer restrictions on the matter of a motherless infant. One year later my mom gave them Ken, too, and then pretty much disappeared to have a different life, with different husbands and different children.

She did visit occasionally, scooping us up for an occasional shopping spree at The Mercantile. Somehow we always ended up drinking cokes at the Oxford, though. But we were doing it in new clothes, by golly. The first time this happened, I remember wondering why it was so dark and smoky and sad in there. I was six years old and I'd never been in bar before.

Dad visited us regularly. We saw him on the major holidays of Thanksgiving and Christmas and also once each summer. He would come, bring us presents, let me read Dr. Seuss to him on his lap, and have great feasts with us. Then he would leave again. One Christmas, he brought us all television sets: a full-size set for my grandparents, a small black Sony for Ken and a small white Sony for me. We thought he was a god.

Sure enough, the day came when my dad remarried and collected up his children. It must've broke my grandmother's heart. We lived in Seattle—I had a mom!—in a new house with a big sister and bedrooms painted the color of our choice. That lasted about a year. They separated, or at least separated from Ken and me; we went back to live with our grandparents. We weren't told why. A year passed and the domestic landscape in Seattle had smoothed itself out, and Ken and I went back, to a new, bigger house in an area called Ballard. I think it was two years later that they finally divorced. My dad held onto to us for another year or so, but frankly, I missed my Gramma. So we finished grade school and then high school in Missoula.

Mom reemerged and reestablished relationships with her two first born, sometimes happy and satisfying, and sometimes full of whiskey and drama. She had demons of her own. She eventually became a strong, sober, resourceful, intelligent woman who volunteered at the Missoula Food Bank. Maybe she felt she had debts to pay. I think regret is payment enough.

My dad stayed close and supportive. He never remarried.

It took some expensive therapy, but over the years I have excised most of my demons and have forgiven the sins of the father and of the mother. I love my parents and I see the past from their individual perspectives with compassion. It takes a certain amount of self-preserving detachment.

By now I was totally depressed and feeling impotent and frustrated in Cairo. I was dreading the Nile cruise, mad that I couldn't just make my own way wherever I wanted to go. I went to the Hilton. The cyber cafe was closed, the delicatessen was closed, Amr wasn't answering his cell phone. All I had to do was sit in the lobby and look miserable.

Thank God for paper and pen. I could literally write my way through my troubles. So I sat for awhile in the lobby, writing, observing. Enclaves of tour groups gathered, talking about the stock market and shopping, anticipating their pre-arranged day. They clutched their *Baraka* water bottles. It looked so easy for them. I had been drinking tap water and trying to pronounce whole sentences in Arabic to people who didn't speak any English.

I was hovering between two worlds: the tourists and the Egyptians. I didn't fit anywhere. And all I wanted at that moment was something over ice. I hadn't seen an ice cube since they were doling them out one at a time in the airplane over Greece. I craved a gigantic tumbler of ice, with juice poured over it. Later Amr told me ice was served only upon request, even with pop and cocktails. Most of the tourists don't want ice, fearing they'll get sick from it.

I sent my father an email when the cyber cafe opened, after I had a big glass of juice (no ice) at the Hilton café. I had very carefully calculated the remaining expenses of my trip. It was midnight in Seattle, Veteran's Day was just beginning and most everyone was asleep. Later that night in Egypt I received his message back: "No problem. $750 in Friday and more available if you need it. Sorry to hear you're off to a rough start. Love, Dad."

No word from James in Luxor. I figured I might as well give up on that and go to Sinai. Amr was arranging a Nile cruise the following week. Things were slowly falling into place.

Waiting for Amr that day in the lobby, I was sitting near a distinguished man in a business suit. When I lit up a cigarette, he pushed an ashtray toward me. "*Shokran*," I said.

"You speak Arabic?" He asked.

"No, no. Only a few words." It was outrageously flattering to think that my pronunciation of the word was remotely authentic. Flattering and delusional—as delusional as a train ride to a remote Egyptian village.

"Where are you from?" he asked politely.

"America."

"Is this your first time in Egypt?"

"Yes."

"Welcome."

"*Shokran*."

"Tell me, why is your Embassy closed today? I had business there, but when I arrived, they were closed."

"It's Veteran's Day," I said. "This is a national holiday, to honor all the veterans who died in all the wars." I flashed on Terry, of course. He died, too. It was almost exactly five years to the day that I had found Terry in his garage, yellow nylon cord around his neck. This is why I can't bear the dark.

That night, back in my room at the Grand Hotel, I was thinking about something Amr had taught me the day before. Muslims pray five times a day to worship Allah, and to thank Him for all He has given them— eyes to see, ears to hear, legs to walk on, the ability to have children. Not all people are given these things. And they thank Allah with grateful hearts for these gifts, and the gift of life itself. All He has given, He will eventually reclaim.

While Muhammad himself was there to supervise the messages that God gave him, what he didn't have was paper. So Muhammad's followers tanned the hides of goats and wrote the sacred words there. And from this came Islam, the last word of God.

It occurred to me that *worship* per se was not so common in America, in my view. We pray to God for blessings and help and advice and guidance and for the healing of the sick. We pray with a list of things we want and think we need. But when do we ever touch our forehead to the ground in *gratitude?* I was deeply moved by the notion of not *asking* for once, to just say *thank you* to God.

So I made a list of that day's gifts from God:

- The traffic policeman in the white helmet, who took my hand and helped me cross six lanes of traffic. Like a waltz we moved together. He would squeeze my hand tightly and pull back on my arm; we would stop in the middle for passing cars. He would relax his grip and guide me forward; we would advance. Not a word was spoken. We danced through 30 cars this way, the dancer and his partner.

- Amr, who arranged so many details of my "impossible" trips to Sinai and Luxor. Amr, who worried. Amr, whose guidance seemed to bestow safety on me. Amr, who taught me how to greet and part with a kiss on each cheek. Left, right, hug. You learn as you go.

- A good hair day.

- Electrobank, which kicked out $300 in cold, hard American cash, with no negotiating. Three crisp, one hundred dollar bills, instant, direct, uncomplicated results, on a day when even getting orange juice was a challenge.

- Dad, for silently worrying, and for planting money in my Panic Fund.

- The hotel employees who always smiled and greeted me warmly, even though I knew it was because I'm a ridiculous over-tipper.

- The doorman of 25 years at the Hilton who remembered my face and my hotel, who had the jet black skin and red in his eyes. I wondered about his past: was he from a titled Sudanese family who lost their fortune to political intrigue, business enemies or bad luck? Or had he raised himself from the streets to earn this snappy uniform and a good day job? What did he quietly think about all the coming and goings of tourists? He was gracious a thousand times a day to a thousand strangers. He holds a vivid and lasting place in my memories.

- The now-familiar divot in my bed, the size of a coffee table, which makes the perfect cave of a writing seat.

- For the toilet paper, which I know will come, eventually, and the fresh towels, no matter how many times I must ask for them.

- For the reservation mistake at the Hilton. I thought I could muster the resources to get a room there despite everything, and an un-opened email was the best my thinking could do. James solved the problem for me, and I couldn't imagine not being at the Grand.

- Tarak, the bartender who remembers me and red wine and always says, "See you tomorrow?"

- The cyber cafe, my one quiet place to reach back home.

- For the exact words in my Arabic phrase-book when I was trying to say, "Can I stay another two nights, please?" to someone who had no English beyond, "Breakfast?"

May I always have so grateful a heart as sits with me this hour, I wrote. I put my forehead on my bed and closed my eyes in gratitude to a God who speaks Arabic.

Chapter Four
The Pyramids of the Giza Plateau: Alone at Sunset

OSIRIS: *Osiris is the god of immortality. God of the dead. God of the living. In a fit of rage, his evil brother Seth hacked him to 14 bits and scattered his limbs all over Egypt. Isis, his beloved, collected these parts and reassembled them. The gods took pity on the passion and devotion of Isis, and resurrected Osiris as the god of the underworld.*

There is something compelling about a person who knows things, who moves and talks in ways that tell you he or she deserves your confidence and your trust. Akmed Noor was one of those people. He took me to the Giza Plateau, the single most popular tourist site in Egypt—possibly the world—where I had the rare opportunity to be there after the monument had closed, virtually alone, at sunset. Akmed Noor, whose name means *bright light*, made it so.

Thursday / November 11 / Giza

Akmed Noor was a guide for hire. I found him at the Nile Hilton, and paid 105 Egyptian pounds (about 30 bucks) for a personal tour of the pyramids. Not a bad deal. I would have Akmed's attention for the entire afternoon and a personal driver to get me to and from the unknown regions outside the city core.

I wonder now about Akmed's past—how he came to be a tour guide—but I never got around to asking him. I like to think that he had an inauspicious start in life, selling cheap bookmarkers on the dirty streets, pestering tourists, and that he ended up graduating summa cum laude in Egyptology from Cairo University. The truth is probably somewhere in between. I'll never know.

If I could go back to Egypt, this minute, I would look up every single person I met and take them to lunch. I was wildly consumed with my own daily needs in Cairo, and I didn't ask enough questions. I needed to listen more, to learn more. Not academically, but personally, one rare, interesting, unique, amazing person at a time.

We got a late start. Our first stop on this particular tour was the Citadel. From here, Cairo spreads itself out toward the horizon. The Citadel itself is a grand, massive structure, built up and added on and lived in by 700 years of Egyptian rulers (from the 12th to the 19th centuries), starting with Salah ad-Din, who chased the upstart Christians out of their/their holy city of Jerusalem in 1187 A.D.

The most imposing aspect of this fortress is the giant dome of the mosque of Muhammad within its walls. Which suggested to me that if Allah was anywhere on this planet, he would surely be there. At least for part of the year. The rest of the months I suspect He needs to get away from it all, at a chalet in Switzerland, perhaps, (sweet, neutral Switzerland), or in a condo on the happy island of Spanish Mallorca.

Would He be there today if I went inside? Would He talk to me if I called His name? Could I lay my sorrows and my regrets at His feet and be absolved of them?

Not today. No time to find out. I had a pyramid to climb and the sun was sinking fast.

Our driver sped us out of the city limits, past incomprehensible road signs written in the beautiful, mysterious Arabic alphabet, along Sharia al-Ahram, 11 kilometers to the Giza Plateau.

We passed school busses coming and going and I have to admit that I was waved to so often and so enthusiastically, I was starting to feel like a famous film star. Living it up while I had the chance, I embraced my fleeting notoriety with aplomb, waving and smiling and blowing kisses. It was that wonderful, blissful feeling of being adored just for showing up. As if being different was suddenly an asset; my oddness was no longer a liability, but rather, a Get Out of Jail Free card.

The Giza district is an 18-kilometer patch of desert on the west bank of the Nile that houses Cairo University, the Cairo Zoo, the luxurious Pyramids Hotel, embassies of France, Israel, Saudi Arabia and Lebanon, as well as a police station and a sound-and-light show worthy of The Rolling Stones. It also offers for sale or rent: clothes, trinkets, papyrus, alabaster, scarves, rugs, tapestries, ceramics, as well as horses and mules, among other things. I didn't see any of it. My eyes were fixed on the monoliths rising over a hundred meters from the desert floor.

By now we were really late. We rushed up to the gates as the monument was closing. Throngs of people were heading out. Akmed and I were jostling our way in. The sun was setting and the sky was turning soft colors of gold. Akmed spoke rapidly to one of the guards and we popped through to the other side. *I was in.*

And there was the sphinx. Just like you see it in movies and pictures, *right in front of me.*

So here was this amazing, mysterious, ancient *thing* that has commanded the attention of poets and philosophers, historians and filmmakers for centuries, and what am I doing? Taking pictures of kids.

Children clustered around me, asking my name, telling me theirs, beaming smiles at my camera, horsing around. The schoolboys were always with a male teacher, and the girls, with their white headscarves, were always with a woman. Others were happily running amuck. They all wanted their pictures taken with me, even the grownups. They said *aloo*, and told me their names one by one.

Slowly, the last of the clusters and crowds dispersed, and were gone. Somehow, through happenstance, great luck, or happy destiny, I was virtually alone at the Great Pyramids at sunset. Only Akmed, who called me *Habibi*, and a few tourist police remained. (*Habibi* means, "one I love." Akmed used it as in, "sweetie-pie," a term of endearment, or warmth.)

Now, the Fourth Dynasty pharaohs—Khufu, Khafre and Menkaure, father, son and grandson—were calling my name. I strode to the ancient pyramid of Khafre.

The stones were soft and cool under my hands. Each limestone and granite block weighs about three tons and fits in precise shape and alignment with the other two-and-ahalf million blocks surrounding it.

The big mystery: *how the hell did they get there?* 4,600 years ago? With no cranes or backhoes? Theories range from intricate engineering schematics, to space aliens, to the prowess of the Atlanteans, who moved the blocks effortlessly with the power of the third eye. I didn't care. It was enough that they were there, silent, haunting sentinels on the ever-shifting sands of time and politics.

I went to Giza to touch the massive stones of these ancient tombs, to lay my hands on the cool blocks, carved by slaves and laborers long-dead, to run my fingers along the incomprehensibly perfect alignments of rock, and to climb the bricked heights to the sky.

Too late. "You cannot climb the pyramid," said Akmed. "It will be dark soon, Habibi. It's too dangerous."

"Oh well, I'll do it some other time. Thanks anyway." The mind plays tricks on you.

What I said wasn't true. When, in this lifetime, would I return to the Giza Plateau? And if I did, how would I get to be there virtually by myself, as the sun turned the sky from white to purple to gold? Answer: Never. I won't. Ever.

In retrospect, I should have insisted. I should have pulled out every pound and piaster in my pockets, along with my three, new hundred dollar bills, to buy my dream from Akmed Noor.

But I wasn't raised that way. I was raised to go along and get along. To be polite. Don't rock the boat. Don't ask. Under no circumstances to demand anything.

A few zillion photographs later, it was time to go.

It was on the way out that I saw the rattletrap settlements—the rickety buildings and dirty streets that were built up around the perimeter of the pyramids to house the children of industry.

In stark contrast to the school children, these children are dirty and thin. They are incessantly pressing tourists to purchase their trinkets. These children, these others of the streets, fed themselves and their families on papyrus bookmarkers and cheap cigarettes. I hated them. I loved them.

Can a woman blow kisses to the little boys, buy ten bookmarkers at a time, give piasters to begging mothers, walk the dirt streets past ramshackle tenement buildings, and not bend with sorrow? Can she not want to rescue them, not weep for them at the end of the day?

Still, I walked away from them, and left them there, unchanged. They, in their innocence and their guilt, changed me.

Another unexpected element of the pyramids tour was a stop on the way back to Cairo at the Papyrus Museum. (Read: retail store for images, large and small, printed on papyrus with the added element of a demonstration of turning plant into paper.) I was there at the very end of the day, alone, and I was expected to buy something. The papyrus demo made use of a tired plant and some water in a bowl and that's all I remember about it. I wandered around the museum taking in images I'd become so familiar with: King Tut's death mask, Nefertiti, Ramses, Isis, and Akhenaten and his wife and daughter offering gifts to Ra.

The call to prayer came and while the storekeepers followed me from image to image (You like this one? It's beautiful, yes?), Akmed Noor excused himself and went to the back of the room to face east, toward Mecca, and pray. I could hear his quiet, gentle chanting as he bent his head to the ground.

It was beautiful. It was important.

Right around this time I stumbled upon a very curious interpretation of the wife and child of Akhenaten: as they presented their offerings to their sun god, they were wearing see-through clothes. I've seen this image a zillion times and believe me, in the original hieroglyphics that survive, these women are wearing linen—modest, reliable linen. For a split second, I felt as though I was in a papyrus porn shop. I wanted to leave. And when Akmed finished his prayers, we did.

Akmed seemed disappointed and confused that I didn't purchase some real papyrus (not the cheap imitation stuff I'd find on the streets). And I was sorry to disappoint him. And I knew I was overreacting. It was just one racy image among dozens of other, truly beautiful ones. But I was done for the day. Akmed took me back to the Nile Hilton and we said goodbye.

I watched him drive away, this young man who spoke four languages, held my camera bag, got me water, and let me be the last of ten thousand tourists who had visited the pyramids that day. Akmed Noor, who had the grace to pray, no matter what else was happening, because his God had called upon him.

It was time for a glass of wine. Aside from the open-air bazaar across from my hotel, the streets in this district housed miles of shops, all bustling with people until late into the night. These Cairo streets stayed alive way past my bedtime: late late. I felt strangely safe out there at night, though, as if the darkness had swallowed up the danger, somehow. As if the lights had gone down on my oddness. As if I belonged.

Finding a bottle of wine wasn't all that hard. Finding a corkscrew was. I went into every shop that had kitchen things and all the stores resembling Rite Aid. I tried to explain what I wanted. Then I tried to draw it. I was odd, again. Different. Out of step. Muslims don't drink alcohol, by the way.

The sin of strong drink outweighs its usefulness, says the Koran. I believe this to be true.

Finally a young man took my hand and walked me out of his store. He led me around corners and past other shops until we came upon a place that had exactly what I needed. *Allah wa Akbar!* (God is great!) A corkscrew.

He smiled and waved and started to walk away. When I held out a gratuity, he refused, saying *afwan, afwan.* It is nothing.

Back in my hotel room, I sipped red wine and wrote copious volumes in my journal. About six pages. I closed the cover, sublimely content with the notion that I had penned the most brilliant and poignant reflections ever conceived on paper regarding Egypt. Then I had some more wine. I didn't know it yet, but in the glaring light of morning those words would fall off the pages and into my lap, as only utter drivel could.

In the meantime, I had only the incessant beeping of the taxicabs outside my window to keep me company. I thought of Mosen Eid and the beat-up cab he drove: the torn seats, loose springs, scrapes, dents, and the lingering smell of cigarettes. His cab spoke of his many days as one of the thousands of cabbies in Cairo. It attested to the highly coveted passengers, the rates he inflated as high as he could, the tips, the streets he drove over and over, and the streets he got lost on. It attested to the long, hot hours, wrestling fares from other drivers, dodging cars, people and goats, and the constant sound of beeping horns that probably never left his head, even when he slept.

Then I had another glass of wine. Tomorrow I would go to Khan el-Khalili, one of the oldest and largest bazaars in the Middle East.

I decided to get my camera ready well in advance of the new day. I had in my possession the greatest roll of film ever taken in all time, at one of the most sacred places on earth, as the sun had changed the world from day to night, and the sphinx had lorded over the ancient landscape. All I needed to do was to rewind the film and tuck it safely into its happy little canister.

How did I do it? I'm still not sure. But in an act of epic stupidity, I exposed inch after inch of raw images to the light and ruined the entire roll of film in one fell swoop.

I thought about the pyramids, sitting in the darkness now, as they have for hundreds of years, through millions of sunsets. They'd be there still, tomorrow, and in hundreds of more years, calm and quiet amidst the chaos of hopes and commerce, secrets and broken dreams.

Allah wa Akbar. I crawled into bed and went to sleep. What else could I do?

CHAPTER FIVE

KNOWING: THE INFINITE GOD

KHNEMU: *Khnemu is the god of creation and fertility and personification of the Nile and its annual flooding. It is said he molded man and the gods on his potter's wheel. His image appeared on Gnostic papyri for three centuries after the crucifixion of Christ. Khnemu Khenti Netchemtchem Anket is a form of this god, meaning: "Khnemu, Lord of the House of Sweet Life."*

Taxi drivers in Cairo want you to remember them. At any cost. So they can charge you pretty much any cost to drive you around. All day. Each day. Anywhere. They act like they love Americans. I wonder. They deserve the inflated fares, I suppose, for running the traffic gauntlet in Cairo hour after hour, day after beastly day, in the heat and the fumes and the beat-up cars whose horns were often the only part working perfectly. One particular day Harbeh was my driver. He promised, "for a very good price," to meet me in between destinations and take me from the Nile Hilton, to Coptic Cairo, to Khan el-Khalili and back to the Grand Hotel. "Call me Harvey," he insisted. Tourists are so vexed in Cairo by the traffic, the language, and the microorganisms in their food, why add to their mayhem with foreign names? Harbeh turned out to be reliable, but only partly so. Like so many people I'd known in my life, he had a way of showing up and a way of disappearing.

Friday / November 12 / The Coptic Museum

First stop: The Coptic Museum. This is an important location in my novel—a site of insidious plots and narrow escapes. That is fiction.

One of the few modern miracles of the Middle East is that—in a region steeped in conflict, bloodshed, and religious fervor—two disparate religious groups have managed to co-exist in relative peace and acceptance, for centuries. The Muslims and the Egyptian Christians. That is fact. At least it was until the 1970s, when sporadic firestorms were ignited by Muslim extremists. The 18-Day Revolution in 2011 didn't help, either.

The *Copts*—Egyptian Christians with roots dating back to St. Mark the Apostle—make up a very small minority of the Egyptian population today, and most of them dwell in the oldest, most conservative part of the city: Old Cairo. Their longevity as one of the oldest institutions of Christianity in the world is due, at least in part, to the Copts' strict and long-held adherence to Jesus' directive to "render unto Caesar the things that are Caesar's, and unto God the things that are God's." The Copts, accordingly, submit to their Muslim rulers, but worship God in their own way. The Coptic Church was never controlled by—or tried in any way to control—the government in Egypt. Which helped their cause enormously.

As my taxi rolled to a stop on the narrow, cobbled streets, I could see ruins from the early Roman Empire near the entrance to the museum. These crumbling stones of once massive columns reminded me of the great history of Egypt, and the many places she had conquered, and times she'd been conquered in return. I paid Harbeh and walked past the ruins, through a tall iron gate, and down a long driveway.

The driveway led to a brick courtyard, flanked by two stone lions. The museum lies within the ruins of the famous Roman Fortress of Babylon. Today it provides a link between ancient Egypt and Islamic Egypt. It also shows the transition from paganism to Christianity, in the formative years of the religion that would become a world power.

There was a food stand outside the entrance and, although I was anxious to see the artifacts, I thought I'd better gather up my wits and my blood sugar so I could give the museum my full attention. I ordered a tomato and feta cheese sandwich and sat under a deliciously fragrant orange tree to eat my lunch. That's when I noticed her.

A little girl of eight or nine was sitting nearby, under a tree of her own, wearing long black braids and an enormous, heartbreaking smile. She should have been in school. She should have been learning to read and write. She should have been playing with dolls. Instead, she was posed, alone, at a table, with a bottle of drinking water. She probably had to sit there for hours, waiting to catch the eye of a tourist, smile and say *aloo*.

Sure enough, I wandered over and asked her if I could take her picture, holding up my camera questioningly. She smiled and glanced over at her parents, who were—surprise—sitting about ten feet away. They nodded and rubbed their fingers together: *baksheesh*, a tip, cash money. Fine. So I'm feeling kind of foolish right about now, but what was I going to do? Walk away and say *no thanks?* Click-click, a few Egyptian pounds, *shokran*.

But get this: while I was off being suckered in by yet another enterprising child, someone stole my sandwich. They *stole my sandwich* three feet behind my back. I swear it's true. There was nothing left to do but go inside the museum. There was something extraordinary waiting there.

After Terry's funeral, in November 1994, I headed home to Montana: the prodigal child, broken, beaten, and lost in a spinning world. The one sanctuary that had been there for me, since I was two month's old and cast from my mother's love, since I was nine years old and left my father's second family, and every Christmas and Thanksgiving that I could remember, was the home of my grandparents.

My Grampa lost his wife only six months prior, and together we made a sad and quiet little duo. I stayed for a month. He helped be re-create my old bedroom with a tiny little bed from a second-hand shop and a mirror on the wall. And then I read. I read and I walked and I watched Star Trek reruns, every day. Every night I cried my self to sleep.

Somewhere, beneath the vines of despair, a bud of hope was growing—something I would be able to cling to and make my own, in time. I had a list of books that I wanted to read and could never seem to get to, so I hauled myself off to the Missoula County Library. Of the 10 books on the list—a list accumulated over time from the bibliographies of other books—I found only one on those library shelves: *The Gnostic Gospels* by Elaine Pagels. What I read in that book blew my holy socks off.

It turns out that in 1947, near a village on the Nile, peasant farmers digging for fertile soil accidentally unearthed a tall jar from the sand. Under cliffs honey-combed with empty tombs, the leader raised his *mattock* (digging tool) and struck open the clay vessel. A plume of gold rose slowly into the air, shimmered in the sunlight, and disappeared. True story. The farmers were awestruck and fearful that they had just released a *jinn*, an evil spirit who would wreak havoc on them. (In truth, the golden apparition came from fragments of 1,600-year-old papyrus, caught in the breeze.)

As they looked down to the remains of the jar, they saw not the treasure that had all hoped for, but rather 13 ancient codices—sheets of papyrus bound into leather covers. They divided the spoils amongst themselves, tearing the covers off of some to more evenly distribute the pages. As the bickering went on and on over who would get what, they eventually decided that the leader, Muhammad Ali al-Samman, would take the whole cache together, sell if for whatever he could, and divide the profits among everyone.

Wait, it gets better, actually worse: Muhammad and his brothers said goodbye to their cousins and friends and headed home to their village in al-Qasr, near Nag Hammadi. Their mother met them at the gate and told them that the murderer of their father had fallen asleep in the roadway with a jar of molasses between his legs. True story. The brothers grabbed their mattocks and trotted out for revenge, leaving the codices by the outdoor cooking stove.

Yes. They did. And yes, *she did.* While her sons were off hacking out the heart of their sworn enemy, and devouring the organ amongst themselves, mom was back home stoking the fire with several sheets of priceless dry papyrus from Christian antiquity.

What they had, and that they didn't realize they had, and what they sold on the black market for a few packs of cigarettes and a crate of oranges, was a library from the Gnostic Christians, penned during the lifetime of Jesus and translated into the Coptic language of the early Egyptian Christians. It was an amazing discovery, rivaling that of the Dead Sea Scrolls in a cave near Qumran, Israel, earlier that same year.

One of the most compelling documents in the Gnostic collection is the *Gospel of Thomas*, 114 sayings attributed directly to Jesus and recorded by Thomas, the once doubting disciple. While I was standing in front of those very pages in the Coptic Museum, in this state of virtual rapture, I hear this man holding forth in the background. I look over to see a big, beer-belly fellow trying to explain the Budweiser frogs to two Japanese tourists. They clearly didn't understand and didn't look like they really gave a crap. They were dying of politeness, and this guy was all over it. I'm guessing his dirty Tshirt, with its blazing beer logo, must have accidentally sparked the conversation.

I was wishing he'd swagger over with a smirk and ask, *So, what does it say?* referring to the tidy, mysterious blocks of Coptic letters on papyrus.

I would have replied, quietly and from memory: *These are the hidden sayings that the living Jesus spoke and Judas Thomas the Twin recorded. And Jesus said, 'whoever discovers the interpretations of these sayings shall not taste death.'* In this way I could have given something back; I could have contributed something.

Scholars believe that these Gnostic codices were omitted from the various texts that became the Bible, because their tenets defied the hierarchy of the church. The Gnostics were labeled heretics and their writings and their societies became secret, or hidden. The capital "C" Church denounced and slandered them. Eventually, the Gnostics vanished from the earth. The discovery of the Gnostic Gospels was a compelling find for Christian history. Finally, the heretics could speak for themselves.

The Gnostic Gospels had a curse on them, however: Jesus said, *'Write down my teachings and keep them in a safe place. Cursed be everyone who will exchange these words for a gift, or for food, or for drink, or for clothing, or for any other such personal thing.'*

Once they were discovered, greed and ignorance kept them hidden from the public for nearly 30 years. The work of James Robinson, of the Institute for Christianity and Antiquity in Claremont, California, was instrumental in seeing these amazing documents published. One of his early students was Elaine Pagels. Through some miracle of fate, her book came into my hands.

A few years later, I would meet Elaine Pagels, whose first husband died in a climbing accident. She called us kindred spirits, women of passion and tragedy.

Back in 1994, I had an idea. This story of the Gnostic Gosepels was ripe for the silver screen. It had all the elements of a blockbuster. So I began to write. I started with a novel, based on the historical discovery, from which I could adapt a screenplay. Every morning, I walked the cold streets of my hometown, block after block, formulating the story in my mind. I had something to hold on to. A thin lifeline back to the land of the living.

The most intriguing thing to me, beyond the buried treasure, blood feud and black market antics, were the *messages* that the Gnostics were spreading: God resided within the *self*. There was a path to the Divine inside each and every one of us, if we had the courage to follow it.

Jesus said, 'If your leaders say to you, look the kingdom is in heaven, then the birds of heaven will precede you. If they say to you, it is in the sea, then the fish will precede you. Rather the kingdom is inside you and it is outside you.

When you know yourself then you will be known and you will know that you are children of the living Father. But if you do not know yourself, then you will dwell in poverty and you are poverty.'

In the introduction to her subsequent book, *Adam, Eve, and the Serpent*, Pagels writes, speaking of an early Gnostic Christian: *Anthony, and others like him, sought the shape of his own soul, hoping to accept the terrors and ecstasies of direct and unremitting encounters with himself, and, having mastered himself, to discover his relationship with the Infinite God.*

That's what I wanted. A relationship with the infinite God. That's why I came to Egypt. That is what brought me to the doorstep of the Coptic Museum and to the golden pages of the *Gospel of Thomas* itself.

I walked right to these ancient pages, behind a Plexiglas case, and quietly wept.

On those long morning walks in Missoula, there was a particular site that I visited every single day. It's a Vietnam memorial, an enormous statue in Rose Park of an angel picking up a fallen solider. Rose Park is just two blocks and a busy street away from my grandparents' house. I used to play there when I was a child. The big draw of the park is the grand display of a wide variety of roses that bloom in the spring and summer. There was a World War II monument in the park when I was little, and over the years memorials were added for the Korean War, the Gulf War, the first Iraq war, and finally the dirty little Vietnam war. It has since been named Rose Memorial Garden.

This place is a sanctuary for me. Always has been, even before I lost my Gramma and Terry. It's a place I go, a touchstone, healing ground. When my grandmother was dying in the hospital earlier that year, I had a spat with one of my relatives and dashed out the back door, crying. When my Grampa went looking for me, he knew I would be in one of two places: The Rose Garden, or the hospital. He found me at my Gramma's bedside, after I'd been to the garden.

So it was to this place I returned every morning that foggy, dismal autumn, to sit, to lament, to pray. Alzheimer's is a terrible thing. It took my grandmother mercilessly. We eventually pulled the plug on her life support and were told she would go in a matter of hours, a day at the most. She languished for five days. Even after she lost consciousness, I held her hand and read to her and talked to her about little things and big things.

It's hard to let go. It's hard to watch someone not let go. It became so painful that most everyone in the family stopped coming to the hospital; the strongest among us wimped out first. Eventually, only my Grampa and I went. It occurred to me more than once, as I watched her suffer and languish, to put a pillow over her sweet face and end it for her, because I loved her so much. Because I believed so fervently that peace, and the people she loved, and the God she prayed to, were all on the other side waiting for her. But I didn't of course. Love has its limits.

I should have been more interested in the other artifacts in the Coptic Museum. Many of them depict the transition of pagan symbols to Christian ones: the ankh becomes the cross. Isis and Horus become the Madonna and Christ child.

But I wasn't interested. I had drunk from the *Gospel of Thomas* like it was a river of cool, clear water and I was full. I wandered in a distracted daze until it was time to meet my cab driver.

Chapter Six
Khan el-Khalili: The Bazaar and the Bizarre

HORUS: *Horus is the hawk-headed god, son of Isis and Osiris, and symbol of healing and universal harmony. Horus lost his eye in a legendary battle with his archenemy, Seth. Wisdom restored it. From this legend, the symbol of a human eye, with hawk-like markings, became an amulet for protection against evil.*

I met Harbeh at the designated hour and overpaid him, again, to take me to the famous bazaar of Khan el-Khalili. Miles of narrow roads were packed with people and bordered by endless rows of shops offering goods and wares, in a collision of art and commerce. The roots of "The Khan" date back to 1382 when, as a medieval spice market and hotel for merchants, it established Cairo as a major center of trade. Today it serves as a popular site for tourists and locals, topped with high-density housing. Gold and silver were for sale in shop after shop that would set my eyes aglow. Strung throughout the myriad alleyways I found onyx, alabaster, ceramics and linens. I also found everything I didn't want to buy: plastic toys, bathrobes, fake alabaster statues, t-shirts, pots and pans, and endless platters engraved with the image of King Tut. (In fact, every possible type of physical item that could have had King Tut's imaged emblazoned upon it, did.) Vendors called out to me, took hold of my hand, offered me things for free, saying, "Come see. Come see." I made a good target, alone and wide-eyed, looking at everything.

Friday / November 12 / Khan el-Khalili

Amidst the noise and chaos of Khan el-Khalili rises the al-Husayn Mosque, one of the most important mosques in Cairo and burial site of The Prophet's grandson, Ibn alHusayn. It was built in 1154, restored in 1236, and then renovated in the early 1900s. Some say it's not accessible to non-Muslims, being one of the most sacred Islamic sites in the Middle East. I stopped in the imposing courtyard and drew a black silk scarf from my backpack. I wrapped it around my hair and approached the entrance. *What was I thinking?* The man at the door motioned me to the other side of the structure. *This must be where they torture infidels who try to enter sacred ground.* Turns out I was at the men's entrance. The women have an entrance of their own. So, if I had to be discriminated against, at least it was for my gender. It seems likely that women in Egypt will embrace birth control and the Equal Rights Amendment long before there is religious peace in this world.

So I let them have their way, took off my shoes, and walked in awe into their holy site. I traded my shoes and *baksheesh* for a little wooden square, a chip of that serves as a claim check for my shoes. Then I stepped onto the softest carpet in the known universe. Not thick, not plush, not colorful, just very, very soft. *How did they do that?*

Women were sitting, some kneeling, some bowing their foreheads to the ground. Some had little children sitting quietly beside them. Prayer time was still a few hours away, so it wasn't very crowded. But the rituals were the same. The prayers begin:

> *Praise be to Allah, Lord of the Worlds,*
> *The Beneficent, the Merciful.*
> *Owner of the Day of Judgment,*
> *Thee alone we worship; Thee alone we ask for help.*
> *Show us the straight path,*
> *The path of those whom Thou hast favoured;*
> *Not the path of those who earn Thine anger nor of those who go astray.*

These first passages of *The Koran*, the Seven of the Oft Repeated, contain within them the essence of the holy book of Islam, without which no prayer is complete.

I moved slowly, as still and unobtrusively as I could. I approached a little side room and watched. Women stood praying at a silver rail. Inside the rail was a wide wooden counter, and I saw a woman put money in a little silver slot. I did the same. Unexpectedly, a man on the corner of the rail handed me a little package. It was a little bitty book, red, with tiny threads of fringe. I didn't dare to open it.

This rail surrounded a huge square box of sorts, made of green glass, and decorated in silver. I had no idea what it was, only that this thing was very important. Women offered their palms toward it, whispering quiet words, some with tears, invoking blessings. Men did the same, on the opposite side of the railing, from another entrance. I didn't go too close, or muscle myself up to the rail. This was theirs.

I wandered back to the main room and found a patch of carpet for myself. This is when I began to weep. What is it about the simple (and terribly complex) act of kneeling before one's God that is so hard? To share this room with women unknown to me, drawn by a religion curious to me, in a building made powerful by the people who came there, plugged me into a collective vein of deep, fragile humanity.

I knelt, I prayed. I took some sweet time to take in all the details of that room, but all I could remember, even a few hours later, was a giant chandelier hanging down from a very high ceiling. That, and the women dressed in black, and the soft, soft, pale green carpet.

I wore the scarf all through Khan el-Khalili as I bought papyrus "good quality" and for me "a fair price," and linens. Somehow I couldn't bear to take the scarf off. It was strange to me, and I can't even say why, but I didn't question it. I just wore it, like I wore my tears in the mosque without knowing why.

Later I learned that the little book was a miniature excerpt of The Koran. The strange green "box" behind the silver rail, was the tomb of Ibn al-Husayn, third *Iman* (honorable leader) of Islam, who died in battle in Iraq in A.D. 680.

An amazing gift, which I found along a deep series of alleys in Khan el-Khalili, was a silver plate. It was embedded with Arabic symbols in gold and copper representing the name of God in different faiths: Islam, Christianity, Judaism, Hindu and Buddhism. It was elegant and beautiful and perfect.

Couldn't it be just that simple? I wondered. Couldn't the religions of the world be arranged like embossing on a plate of precious metals, bending to the Artist's imagination? Couldn't the denominations, faiths, sects, tribes, anti-faiths, pagans and princes co-exist in this kind of elegant artistry, to be admired and respected as whole?

In the coming years: the Cole and its crew were attacked in a Yemen harbor; airplanes made of human torpedoes slammed into the World Trade Center, the Pentagon and the hard Pennsylvania ground; foreign nationals were beheaded on Al-Jazeera television; innocent Muslims were beaten on American streets; bombs rained down on Afghanistan; tanks rolled into Baghdad; nightmares unfolded at Abu Graib and Guantanamo; Hezbollah militants attacked Israeli soldiers at their northern border; Israel destroyed southern Lebanon.

There would be no peace among religions.

I continued to wander though Khan el-Khalili, mostly lost among the people, looking now for a restaurant called El-Dahhan. Amr had insisted I go there for *kebab* and *kofta*. He wrote it down for me in my journal: "1/4 of a kilo." I didn't know what this was, but I trusted Amr completely. The next big problem was how, in this sprawling labyrinth of commerce, and no street addresses, would I possibly find it?

Right about then, a particular young shopkeeper called out to me. His smile was wide and friendly. I opened my journal and asked about el-Dahhan, showing him what Amr had written in Arabic. He pointed and directed me in English to the restaurant. It turns out I was about 20 yards away from it. *How could that possibly have happened?*

"You must come back, though," urged the shopkeeper, who had done me a favor. "Come back for one American minute. And because you are so beautiful, a free gift." I promised I would return.

El-Dahhan has been at Khan el-Khalili for decades. And decades and decades. It's famous for kebob, and you can believe it. Smoke pours out the front of the open building. Men sit at the counter amidst the smoke and the hustle of the cooks, eating and talking. Happy, noisy diners filled three storeys of el-Dahhan, and I was led to the top floor. I was thankful to notice that the billowing smoke didn't reach these heights, except for in the smell of the roasted meat.

I stood around for a few minutes, looking, waiting. All the people appeared to be locals; they knew what they were doing. I was odd-man-out again. There was no host or *maitre' d*. Finally someone pointed me to a table. Happily, I knew just what to order. Amr, my best newest friend on the globe, had given me specific instructions. Which was a good thing, because there were no menus lying around. And they would have been written in Arabic if there had been. "Kafta and a quarter kilo of kebob, please." I was able to say this with some authority, though I had never ordered anything by the kilo before. It sounded exotic and dangerous, like something out of *Miami Vice*. I also ordered a Pepsi. I had quit drinking soda pop over a decade earlier, but I wanted to take a picture for a friend in Seattle, who worked for Pepsi-Cola. Photographing food in Khan el-Khalili raises some eyebrows, I can tell you that. I was learning to shrug and smile. I am who I am.

A waiter also brought me bottled water, a plate of creamy hummus, pita bread and a third plate of the wonderful combination of chopped tomatoes, cucumbers, lettuce, onions and . . . well . . . stuff. This was *kafta*. Shortly after came a quarter-kilo of deep-flavored, kebab: four pieces of chopped meat, pressed on a skewer and roasted for about 600 years. There was so much food on my table by this time, I ate less than half of everything they brought me.

Part of the extreme disappointment of the Terrible Camera Tragedy—besides destroying the greatest roll of film ever taken at the pyramids at sunset—is that now I was a *tourist*. I was a tourist with a little, black, point-and-shoot flash box. I had pictured myself as a traveler, a photo-journalist, finding the perfect compositions, capturing just the right light, immortalizing images on film. (Forget for a second that I have not the slightest skill or natural propensity at photography, whatsoever.) With my big camera and telephoto lens, I was an Important Person, taking serious photographs. Now, I was just another tourist snapping pictures. Like the one I took of my lunch at El-Dahhan, while the waiter rolled his eyes to the heavens.

Then I had a promise to keep. The shopkeeper across the street sat me down and served me hot, absurdly sweet tea. We spent an hour together, Zahur, his two brothers, and me. They showed me many different things, trying to figure out what I would buy. How much I would pay.

I started with a delicate glass container, as well as perfumed oil to put in it. Using the back of his hand, Jahur rubbed the heady, scented oil on to my wrist. It was as delicate and intricate as a fragile glass bottle, this buying and selling of goods in Khan el-Khalili.

I also selected a small silver pendant of the Eye of Horus. Zahur said Horus was the god of love. Which was not true. But I can understand why he said it. A woman traveling alone without a wedding ring must surely need help in the Love Department. I bought the amulet.

Horus and his eye represent an important part of Egyptian lore. Though the tales vary in many details, the gist of it is this: Horus was the son of Osiris and Isis. Seth (the dastardly god of darkness) was his brother and arch enemy. They battled again and again for the right to the throne of Egypt. Their legendary fights include: incarnating as hippopotami to see who can stay under water longer; a boat race with one ship made of wood, the other of rock; a good deal of interference from Isis, who favored Horus; and a semen fiasco that I won't get into here. In one episode, Seth cuts out Horus' eye. Some versions of the myth say that Thoth, the god of wisdom, restored it. Others say it was Hathor, who healed both eyes with the milk of a gazelle. In any case, Horus regained his sight and was eventually crowned king of Egypt.

Together, these brothers symbolize the eternal strife in the universe between good and evil. The eye of Horus represents healing, universal peace and protection against evil. I wore this amulet around my neck for the next many years, adding it to a necklace of my own that I had made specifically for this trip.

That necklace contained a luminous, golden-brown piece of quartz called a tiger's eye, which I had been given as a gift some years prior. Before I left for Egypt, I had this gemstone mounted in a gold setting and hung on a chain. On the back of the setting I had the words *ma'as salama* inscribed, meaning, *go in safety.*

I put the Eye of Horus on the same chain as the tiger's eye, the gold and silver together (a fashion *faux pas*), and wore this talisman throughout Egypt. I wanted to believe it protected me. I can tell you there were times when I rubbed the stone furiously, as though to conjure a genie from these ancient lands. As if Isis herself might appear on my behalf, as she had for her son. A mother's love is not something I had known much of, so it was hard to imagine. As hard to imagine as the magical protection of icons in silver and gold. But I did come out of the whole affair unscathed, didn't I?

The sun was setting when I left the last shop, and I was drained. It was time to meet Harbeh by the banana tree next to the mosque. Walking out along many more streets—crowded with people and complicated by an occasional car, bike, cart or motorcycle—someone said to me, "Surprising how quiet Cairo is." I smiled.

I liked Ahmed instantly. He was slender and slight, with glasses, a cotton shirt and perfect English. But I shrugged him off, taught to be cautious, and to avoid strange men in particular. This man walked along beside me for awhile, a pace or two away in the crowd, chatting with me. This was another improvised dance. He would move forward and then wait a bit, to see if I would meet up with him. Then he would take stride with me and make conversation.

Ahmed was friendly and was easy to be with. I was happy to let go of my suspicions—which were largely imposed on me by guidebooks—and pleased to relax and simply enjoy his company. When I stopped to take a picture, I asked him to wait. I wanted to walk with him some more, comfortable in three minutes' time. A dance is like that. He waited, and we walked on.

Negotiating foot traffic and zealous vendors in Khan el-Khalili is one thing. Automobiles are something else entirely. How they even make it through the crowds would amaze you. They go slowly, but not that slowly. This is how I found myself and my backpack of treasures wedged in between a moving truck loaded with cotton, and stack of wooden crates outside a store. Ahmed and other walkers had slid through the narrow openings on each side of the truck like it was just another person on the streets. I got stuck, and was being squished as the truck rambled through, unaware that I was there. My body was about to be broken flat, rendered like an old cardboard box. "Ahmed!"

Ahmed saw what was happening and cried to the driver, "Watch out! Watch out!" Then, without waiting for the truck to stop, he grabbed my hand and pulled me from harm. I was grateful. I was embarrassed.

Call out or be squished: that is what I learned in Khan el-Khalili that day.

I'd been squished before. I'd been ground down, shaped, changed until—looking ahead from the past—I didn't recognize myself anymore. It had happened over time, while no one, not even myself, had been watching.

I didn't come to Egypt to recover lost parts of myself. But those parts found me. Like I called out to Ahmed, and Ahmed shouted to the driver, there are times when it is urgent to call out. To be loud. To demand change. I was finding my way back to myself.

"Thank you," I said to Ahmed. "*Shokran. Shokran.*" Even though Ahmed spoke perfect English, I now had a familiar habit, a word of thanks to the Egyptian people.

We walked on. Soon we came to the promised spot where I would meet Harbeh. Five o'clock sharp. How I managed to arrive exactly on time, I cannot guess. But my driver wasn't there.

I said good-bye to my newest friend and he walked away. That's when the trouble began.

For Harbeh, being late by even 30 seconds, could mean a missed opportunity. You just can't stand still in Cairo for long without something happening. Sure enough, a young man approached. "You waiting?"

"Yes. I'm meeting a taxi."

"Where?"

"Right here. Across the road." I pointed to the bananas. "There."

"What time?"

"Now. Five o'clock." I pointed to my watch.

"Where are you going?"

"Nile Hilton."

"*Nil Hilton?* No problem. Come with me. I'll get you a taxi." He took my arm and started leading me away.

I faltered, looking back for Harbeh. 5:03 P.M. It wasn't so long to wait, given the streets, crowds and traffic he had to battle to get there. If he'd come early, there would be no parking or loading zone where he could wait for me. And I had promised him I'd be there.

"Come. come. The taxi is just down here." The young man was soon flanked by two others, and they talked rapidly to each other in Arabic.

I stopped walking, looked back for Harbeh, and looked again at my watch.

Out of nowhere, Ahmed appeared. "Your taxi didn't come?"

"No."

Ahmed intervened, talking easily to me in English, to the young men in Arabic. Finally he said, "Five o'clock? What don't you just wait a few minutes."

We all stood around together and acted like old pals. I took Ahmed's picture. One man took a picture of Ahmed and me.

"Are you friends with these people?" I asked Ahmed.

"No. People just meet each other this way in Cairo."

For the difference between one cab and other, and the value of three dollars, I would have preferred this all be settled easily. It was not.

Ahmed soon suggested we walk. "It's difficult to find a taxi right here," he said. "It's easier out on the street." He walked me quickly down the alley toward a busy street.

I heard the young men speaking angrily at Ahmed, approaching fast from behind. When the leader of the three put on strong hand on Ahmed's neck, I called out, "Hey! Stop that!"

Everyone smiled, like we were all friends here. But three whole dollars were at stake. We were not all friends here.

Ahmed was trying to find me a safe, fair cab ride out of the bazaar. I didn't understand it all at the time, and it happened so quickly. I was getting scared.

One of the other young men struck up a conversation with me, while the leader walked step for step with Ahmed. I hastened my step to catch up with Ahmed, fearing for his safety.

"Is everything okay?" I asked.

"Yes. No problem," Ahmed replied.

Still, I worried. Would they beat him up? What did he know about these men that made him want to find me another cab? Where would he go from here?

A black and white taxi eased along beside us on the street. Ahmed called to the driver and spoke to him in Arabic. Ahmed opened the back door for me and I sat down, gratefully, in the back seat.

But it wasn't finished yet. The three men were bargaining with the driver from the other side of the car. "Pay him in advance," said Ahmed smoothly. I stepped out of the cab, digging into my backpack for my wallet. "Relax," said Ahmed. "He will wait for you."

A ten-pound note pressed into the driver's hand settled the affair, and I turned to Ahmed. Are you okay? Are you sure you'll be okay? "Yes, yes," he replied. I waved good-bye. Good-bye forever. *Ma'as salama*, Ahmed. Go in safety. I prayed it to be true even as the taxi pulled away, and the crowd behind me dispersed.

I worried that Ahmed would be hurt by those men. I wondered why I didn't have the grace or presence of mind to offer him a ride in my taxi, at least a few safe blocks away. I would never see him again. I would never know. And it ate at me.

Until I saw him again, three days later.

I had barely just arrived back at the Nile Hilton from Sinai when I heard a soft whistling sort of call. Then a voice behind me: "Kyla!" It was Ahmed. I was jubilant to see him. We sat and talked for a few minutes and he assured me that he had been just fine after the incident at the bazaar.

"I'm so glad to see you!" I said. "So relieved that you're all right." Then, "What are you doing here?"

"I came to change money from my American account," he explained. "I came in one door and just, all of a sudden, decided to leave by another door. And there you were."

"It was lucky for me to see you here," I said.

"God has written it," he replied, drawing on his hand with his finger. "It was planned."

Being in a foreign country required a zillion little decisions on matters that I took for granted back home in Oregon. Simple things that I didn't know any more: how to get a table, pay now, pay later, seat yourself, find a waiter, pay more, bargain longer, offer a ride, talk to a stranger, run. You learn as you go. But I was starting to get accustomed to the strangeness of it. It started to fit.

I eventually became most amazed by the things I saw which were strange to Egypt. Not strange *in* Egypt any more, or *about* Egypt, but strange from the Egyptian prospective. It's the things that are foreign to *them* that I started noticing the most. Like the Budweiser guy, for example. 'Nuff said about him. Then there was the teenage American girl in the tight clothes flirting in the 16-year-old high school way with the guy who ran the Internet cafe. He was probably 25 or 30.

Then there was the woman in a skimpy black skirt and pants accessorized with gold lamé purse, belt and shoes wearing screaming red lipstick at the bazaar, amongst Muslim women draped head to toe in tents of black. I saw young men in Tevas and shorts walking through the Hilton like they were on spring break in Miami, and a blonde woman in a slinky sleeveless dress buying a Coke in Old (read: extremely conservative) Cairo.

They offended me somehow. Maybe because I brought all sweaters and baggy pants, and it was hot all the time. Maybe it's because I was trying harder. Maybe it was a respect of place and culture. Maybe, even though they took our money happily, the Egyptians were secretly offended by all of us. And I knew it.

This might be a good time to mention tourists in general. In general, I started to despise them. For one thing, the Americans I saw coming and going at the Hilton seemed unscathed, untouched by being in a third world country. For me, everything seemed hard. While it probably wasn't entirely true, they seemed to breeze through their days, piece of cake, while I struggled.

I was always caught between two worlds, belonging to neither. I had a profound respect for the culture of the country I was visiting. Even though their practices seemed odd, antiquated, even backward in some ways, who was I to judge? I'm not a nation builder. I'm a traveler, a visitor, a guest.

And yet, I didn't belong there. I never would. I found comfort in this in-between place one person at a time. Making friends out of strangers, in random chaotic encounters.

Now might be a good time to talk about women in Egypt: They are gorgeous. And not. Stylish, and not. Whiskered. Elegant. Progressive. Downtrodden. Ephemeral. Mysterious.

Amr said that before Islam, women were treated a possessions, used for pleasure and family matters, looked down upon. Allah elevated women as equal to men, to be respected. He asked that they respect themselves. The most conservative women dress in the black veil and *chador*. God, they must be hot. These were mostly older women, who had dressed this way for security and protection all of their adult lives, and had no interest in getting caught up in the offensive notions of western sensibilities.

A person can look at a woman like this and decide that her customs are demeaning to her. Archaic. Mean-spirited, even. One could also look at a wet T-shirt contest in rural America and think the exact same thing. The root, the intention of all this covering up, is one of modesty, of self-respect. The practice, in my eyes, seems to belong somewhere in the Dark Ages, but in essence, I get it.

I think of young American women, girls really, with their thong underpanties peeking out of their low-rise jeans, and I get it. I think of their push-up bras shoving every possible molecule of flesh outside their tank tops, and—dare I say it?—I get it. I understand the notion, the impetus—if not the *chador*—of self-respect.

Then there's the modern interpretation of the head covering: the silk scarf. Put any one of these women in a convertible on Rodeo Drive in Beverly Hills and you have yourself a dark-haired Paris Hilton. These were beautiful, elegant women, not the marginalized chattel of western imaginations.

The most liberal application of the head covering was a simple headband. I didn't see this very often and only on the most progressive of women. Practical, intelligent—a nod perhaps to the old customs—but definitely in the spirit of change.

I loved the ingenuity of it all. I loved seeing the evolution of the head covering, as women applied modern tastes to age-old rituals. I loved that all three applications coexisted happily together. To each her own.

CHAPTER SEVEN
DAHAB: THE PROMISES OF TRAVEL

KHONS: *Khons, the moon god, is the wanderer or traveler. His name means navigator and he is best known as a god of healing. He wears a crown of the crescent moon cradling the full moon. He is also known as Khensu Nefer-hetep, who possessed absolute power over the evil spirits of earth and air and water.*

I was unprepared for Sinai. That shield of land wedged between Egypt and Israel: an emptiness covered from one coast to the other with mile after mile of nothing but hot dry sand, and then more sand; a strategic piece of real estate won hard and fought over often; its canal the shipping route of war and commerce; a coastline rich in marine life, coral reefs, pristine waters and European tourists; the land of Moses and the Ten Commandments, and the great parting of the sea by the hand of God.

Saturday / November 13 / Dahab

Sinai: I was unprepared.

But that didn't stop me from taking the bus from Cairo to Dahab. That didn't stop me from a ten-hour trip through the desert from the noisy, frenetic crowds of the great city on the Nile to the muted resort village on the southeast coast of the peninsula. Despite Amr's dire warnings of hardship, I would go. For me, this was a quest, an odyssey, things to learn, my own personal exodus to the Promised Land of inner peace. Besides, how hard could it be? I'd catch the bus at midnight, sleep through the night and brunch in Dahab by the beach on fresh fruit, a made-to-order omelet, and chocolate-filled pastries. The word *hardship* was certainly exaggerated, a subtle misnomer created by the language barrier.

I had things to learn on Sinai.

I threw everything I thought I'd need for two days and nights into my leather backpack: a change of underwear, a toothbrush, cigarettes, passport, cash, my journal. I was to climb Mt Sinai, and what I took with me, I would carry up 2,600 vertical feet. And back down. So I was traveling light—without the highly coveted blow-dryer for my hair, without my Lewis N. Clark Model DK2000 Dual Converter with Adapter Plugs, without a jacket, without a change of clothes. I did pack lipstick, though. It weighs almost nothing. And moisturizer, of course. And, according to lifelong instructions from my grandmother: a cotton handkerchief.

The open-air bus depot in Cairo at midnight should have been a sign that this trip was a very bad idea. But I only ever look for good omens. I look for the omens that verify my current thinking. Bad ones I ignore, because I don't want to change my mind. Besides, I was getting used to being afraid.

The fact that the bus depot scared me—with its dirt and litter and quiet, waiting men—didn't stop me. Oh, no. I had a front row ticket to Sinai. And life must be like an E Ticket at Disneyland, mustn't it? Safety comes guaranteed with your ticket price, right? It was later that night, in the middle of God-forsaken nowhere, that I would question this attitude sincerely, and perhaps for the first time in my life.

I rode that bus through a Middle Eastern Twilight Zone. Aside from the loud woman-beater movie that played on video screens suspended from the ceiling; aside from the solemn passport police, boarding every few hours to study dark solitary faces, faces holding secrets, secrets wanting to be kept; aside from the co-driver who did nothing but chain smoke under the *No Smoking* sign for ten straight hours; aside from all this, I was sitting next to a terrorist. More precisely: a really creepy guy had stolen my neighbor's seat, and plopped himself down next to me.

The bus had stopped in el Tur, a southern village towards the tip of Sinai. People disembarked in droves to smoke cigarettes. Not seeing a women's room in the outdoor bus stop, I opted to stay on board. Suddenly, from the back, a man approached. Dressed in a bulky, white jacket, he came forward, stopped at the vacated seat next to me, paused, smirked, and sat down. *He sat down.* Next to me. Bus seats in Egypt are *assigned.* That seat was *taken.* And I was suddenly so unhappy. Convinced he had a long thin stiletto hidden in the bulk of his soiled jacket, I began to look around the bus for some sign of support, or help. That was when I noticed that I was the only women on the entire bus. And only one of two of Caucasians. As if skin color should matter. Suddenly, though, it did. And it wasn't helpful at all that the one and only white guy on the bus had the gnarliest dreadlocks I'd ever seen.

When the other passengers returned to the bus, seeing what had happened in Row One/Seat Two, they began to scold the nasty seat-usurper, one after the next as they walked by. I had no idea what anyone was saying, and it occurred to me that they actually might be encouraging him. But it seemed more like scolding.

Creepy Man, in return, merely shrugged and shook his head. But he couldn't manage to look innocent. And he wasn't about to budge. I put my backpack on my lap as a shield, and turned on my little overhead reading light, so there could be a witness.

I vowed to stay awake the rest of the night, watching this man, so that he knew that I knew, and that no matter what happened, I was watching.

I was never supposed to leave Missoula. I was supposed to marry Gary, graduate from the University of Montana, raise two kids and teach elementary school for the rest of my life.

But life had other plans for me. Blame it on the IRS. That and the fact that my parents married young and divorced worse for the wear. With their whole lives still ahead of them, they left the task of raising their two children to others. My grandparents did a loving job of it, with some financial support and semi-annual visits from my father, who ensconced himself a safe distance away in Seattle.

All this family drama trickles down to one salient point: out-of-state tuition. It turned out that I would have to pay much higher, non-resident tuition to attend the University of Montana—in my own hometown, where I was born and mostly raised and earned $1.85 an hour in high school at Hermes' Holiday Drive-In (Home of the Bonus Burger). But my father had been claiming his two children as dependants on 18 years of income tax returns.

Bam! I was registered at Washington State University—located in Pullman, halfway between my grandparents and my dad—faster than you could say "Tuition Appeal Form." I was away from home and without supervision for the first, thrilling, unexpected time in my highly sheltered life.

I believe that college helped shaped my future. Who I met, where I went, the person I became—everything downstream of that college application was different than it would have been if I'd stayed home. I'm sure of it.

Still, how I got from the Home of the Bonus Burger to a midnight bus on Sinai remains a mystery to me.

When I woke it was dawn. When I slept it was almost dawn. I was beyond tired. I mustered up the courage to ask the chain-smoking co-driver, "What time to Dahab?" pointing at my watch. He paused his conversation with the driver long enough to tell me, "No, this bus doesn't go to Dahab. It goes to Sharm el-Sheikh."

"No," I stated clearly, as only someone with an E-Ticket to Disneyland can do. "This bus goes to Dahab." He shook his head. "Sharm el-Sheikh." (Sharm el-Sheikh—known as the City of Peace, for the many international peace conferences hosted there—would make the news on July 25, 2005, when three car bombs leveled several hotels there, killing 75 tourists and wounding 200 more, in the bloodiest terrorist attack in Egypt in eight years.)

Dawn had lit the Sinai mountains and gave rise to hope in me, dissipating the fears of the night. But this was unhappy news. I had to take Bus Number Two to Dahab. Here's the thing about that: you just never know if there *is* a Bus Number Two. Or if you'll find it. Or if it will cost more money that you don't have. Or when it will leave. The notion of being stranded in a bus depot, language-challenged, on the Red Sea, is not a comforting one.

As it turned out, though, the transfer was quick and easy and in about an hour, I was plunked down in another world altogether.

Dahab was clean and muted, starkly quiet compared to the constant, frenzied noise of Cairo. Standing at the manicured gates of Novotel Dahab felt strangely safe and surreal. Resorts are built gracefully in Dahab, low and slopping gradually from the beach toward hills of sand and stone. Flags crack in the wind bearing the insignias not of nation states, but of diving companies. The bungalows are small and inviting, little globes of sweet respite, in two-by-twos along the pathway.

People come from around the world to dive and windsurf this pristine area on the Red Sea. Cairo to Dahab is like going from Hell to Club Med—a warm oasis spun in shades of blue and green and sand. I stood in the still, dry air at the gates of the resort, a lush garden courtyard stretching in front of me, in quiet amazement. I would spend two days there, in a cottage on the beach.

First stop: breakfast. I found myself in a happy enclave of European pleasure seekers, which took some getting used to. *Where did all the white people come from?* We were collected in an open-air restaurant, a huge breakfast buffet spread out before us, the blue and bluer waters just beyond, and terracotta-colored mountains lining the horizon. My ten-hour bus nightmare was over and everyone there was looking healthy and tan, clad in shorts, thongs, tank tops and T-shirts. It was if I had wandered through the back of the wardrobe into the Narnia of the Red Sea.

Immediately before me: a warm croissant, baby donut and juice that tasted like Tang. I could walk five yards away from my backpack and not have an anxiety attack. I tried to make myself eat some breakfast, which would cost 24 pounds ($8) that morning, because *my* complimentary breakfast would come the *next* morning. But I'd be on the mountain the next morning. Nothing came easy. But it was so quiet there, nothing seemed to bother me. I felt better than I should have. Still, I couldn't seem to make myself eat anything. I thought to negotiate my breakfast bill— *who cared if I ate my one complimentary breakfast today or tomorrow?*—but it was worth $8 not to have to talk to anyone at the moment. My room wouldn't be ready until noon, and the beach was calling, "Kyla, Ky-laaaa."

This is when I learned the terrible news: I had unwittingly arrived on the wrong day. I had to be back in Cairo before the next tour bus went to Mount Sinai, and I would miss my one and only chance to walk in the footsteps of Moses. I had come so far to climb the rugged mountain, hear the pilgrims chant, and touch the face of God. And I was a day too early.

Discouraged and drained, I sat down on a beach chair and cried into my sweater. I thought I could arrange my trip to St. Catherine's Monastery (Mt. Sinai's base camp) *after* I got to Dahab. I had one day to get to the mountain, the night to climb it, the morning to watch the sun rise, a moment to have my big epiphany, one day to get back to Dahab, and another day to get to Cairo. That's one day more than I had, because no one would take me to the mountain on Saturday night. The monastery was closed to the public on Sunday. No trip. No way. No how. I would sit in Dahab for a day, and then return to Cairo on the bus, empty-handed.

The tourists at Dahab Novotel were mostly German, mostly serious, not particularly friendly, and one hundred percent intent on water sports. I didn't hear any laughter in 36 hours. I saw mostly men, tanned, in many shapes and sizes, all wearing Speedos. There were women, too, fewer though, in the same shapes and sizes, strolling the beach in bikinis. I was wearing the same long pants, cropped shirt and sweater I'd worn the day before, and would wear again tomorrow. I must have been an apparition to the others, gathered there for a different purpose. They all looked at me with strange, curious expressions. Maybe it was because I was the only person on the beach, possibly the entire coastline, not wearing a swimsuit or a wetsuit. Maybe it was because their faces all tilted to the sun to gage the gentle winds, and mine as a mask of gloom. Maybe it was my hair.

I heard the call to prayer, at its regulated times of day, entirely ignored by most travelers here. I imagined, though, in some quiet place hidden from tourists, someone moving quietly. Someone moving with intent, to remove his shoes, to kneel to the ground, to dip his head before Allah, to worship.

I thought of Amr. He was going to call me at the hotel at noon the next day to check on me. I didn't want to have to tell him that my great quest had failed. His heart would break for me. It was he who made this journey more a wonder than a disaster, more possible than impossible. An over-booked hotel suddenly had a bungalow available on the beach, "in favor of Miss Merwin," with a late checkout, for 40 U.S. dollars, including tax, confirmed in advance, via fax.

So, if a wayward traveler ever crosses my path, or if I see a woman crying alone on a happy beach, I'll take pains. Amr, by his example, says it must be so.

Sad, longing music wafted through the wind, originating in the Sunset Bar. I took it with me as I walked along the beach, odd man out again. Saudia Arabia was just across the water. I could see it. Miles of coastal reefs beckoned scuba divers like sirens. *What was I doing here?*

Flying by night to Chicago, the first waypoint on my trip to Egypt, I was letting my fears bubble up inside me with great gusto, leaking into every corner of my mind. I was wondering then, and again on the beach that day, if perhaps my dream was too big.

Then came the moment. At some point in my despair, a thin ribbon of hope offered itself up. Tears stopped short in the birth of a new idea. Help came from the movies. I had learned from Hollywood how to solve my problem, because I had learned from the movies how to make a *bribe*.

I've been told there are two types of people in this world: Rule Followers and Rule Breakers. I had always, *always* been a Rule Follower, a Goody-Two-Shoes, naïve. Now I was going to bribe an Arab tour operator named Salém.

I called him through the hotel operator and asked him to meet me by the pool. If I could find a way to get directly from St. Catherine's to Cairo, without returning to Dahab first, I could make my trip to the mountaintop. I shoved a loose 20-pound note in my pocket for easy access. (I once gave a 10-pound note to a man who poured me tea and smiled when I asked for an ashtray, because one was sitting right in front of me. So if Salém could fix my passage back to Cairo, I could spare 20 pounds. No problem.)

"Skip the mountain altogether," advised Salém, who had a sleeve-full of other tours he could offer me.

"I have to go to the mountain," I replied. "I *have* to go to the mountain." Eventually, and for 140 Egyptian pounds (about 41 dollars), the deed was done. Salém arranged a van to take me from Dahab to Mount Sinai and from there, another van to take me directly to Cairo, solving my dilemma.

This is one of the promises of travel: you will no longer be quite yourself when you return. You've pushed yourself beyond your limits. Little by little, you become more than you thought you were.

Before I would reach Mount Sinai, there were other journeys to take, however. And Dahab had gifts for me.

My first night in Dahab, I ate at an outdoor Italian restaurant on the beach. I was the only person in the room beside the waiter, Ebrahim. Ebrahim explained that all the tour groups ate at the main banquet room, together. The buffet came with their lodging. I ate lasagna, alone, and wrote about my day. I felt raw, as if I'd bled my guts all over the Sinai landscape in less than 24 hours. I thought God must be making me tender, carving open my heart for the days to come. By nightfall, I found myself content, and not afraid.

Ebrahim became my only friend in Dahab. He was sweet and shy, and worried that I didn't eat enough. The following day I heard him call to me: "Hello!" He looked happy. "Play volleyball?" I declined, too shy, too used to being alone. "Come on! It's free. Come play."

Suddenly I was joining something, which felt odd and tenuous and surprising. I dropped my backpack in the sand and my shoes by a palm tree, and joined. I was now speaking the international language of sport. Competition has its own vernacular and its own spirit: trying, clapping, shrugging, shouting, awkward team efforts, skin-on-that, smiles and disappointments. Twelve odd players: German, Arab and one American. I never understood the score. When it came my time to serve, I simply called out, "Okay!" They all called back, "Okay!" and on we played.

Ebrahim was a very good player, though most of the rest of us were not. "Keep it," he would say, handing me the ball for my turn to serve. Meaning, *keep the ball, make the point, do good.* He wanted to win. Our team lost three times on a row. But I played hard, and happy to. When it was over, a middle-aged woman in a T-shirt and bikini bottoms, who was unmistakably the worst, happiest player of all of us, asked me to play again tomorrow, at four o'clock. "I'm sorry. I'll be in Cairo tomorrow." I pointed to my watch. "Oh, so sorry," she replied.

Ebrahim also came up and asked, as I collected my shoes and backpack, "Tomorrow? Four o'clock?" "No. I'll be in Cairo by then." I pointed to my watch again. *Why did I always do that?* Time, I guess. Time would take me away. "Oh, that's too bad," he said. I shook his hand. "*Shokran. Shokran.*" Sometimes you want to say the words out loud, even though no one understands them: *Thank you. It was nice to be asked to join. Thank you very much. You understand?*

That night I ate dinner with Ebrahim. Again, I was the only guest in the warm, breezy outdoor restaurant. It was against the rules for him to sit with me, but I asked him, and he did. We talked carefully, Ebrahim struggling with English. I told him I was going to Sinai later that night; how this was a very special place in Christianity and Judaism; how important it was, inside, to be going there. I touched my hand to my heart.

Ebrahim told me about Alexandria, his home, and how he missed his family: mother, father, three brothers and two sisters. He invited me to visit his parents in Alexandria. "You would like the Mediterranean," he said. "I know because I saw you earlier. You look out to the sea, and then you write in your book." He seemed homesick. I understood, but in a different way. I do not yearn for my family when I'm absent. On this trip though, I longed for things like ice cubes and *maitre 'ds.* I longed for simplicity.

Ebrahim would be back in Alexandria the following week. I should call him, he said, if I want to go there. *Who wouldn't want to go to Alexandria?* Who wouldn't want to stand at the shores of the Mediterranean and look northward, as Cleopatra did, waiting for Caesar, and then Marc Antony, to return to her? "If I can make it Alexandria, I will call you," I said. "We'll drink red wine by the sea."

"It's only two hours by train from Cairo," he explained.

I would not go. Time would take me elsewhere.

Radwan wore a black Harley Davidson T-shirt stretched tight over his muscles. I met him at the Sunset Bar. He had oil on the back of his hand. Now *that* was interesting. "I am the masseuse here," he said. *Brother, am I happy to meet you!* For half an hour Radwan spread oil and warmth over by body: my back, arms, neck and face. There is something so soothing about touch and the attention of hands. I'm speaking professionally now, in terms of a masseuse to a traveler who slept the previous night sitting up, fearing for her life. Reedy Egyptian music played softly in the background, while I floated out of my body and away from weightier concerns. I surrendered to the delicious indulgence of the cool, dim, hut, sequestered in someone else's care, away from the glaring brightness of day.

There was oil on the door handle of the massage hut where Radwan worked. It made me smile, this simple thing: the remnant of one man's work, going along with him on his hands, staying behind. I can smell it still, some moments, on the salty air: the scent of jasmine. It takes me back to Dahab and the Red Sea, and a beach made lonely by the crowds.

When the storm of tears passed that first morning in Dahab, and I started concocting a plan, good things happened. Things were really going quite well; I just didn't realize it. I was reminded of faith in life as it is. Tearful and disillusioned when things didn't go my way, I let everything look impossible. Extraordinary things would eventually come out of all the disappointments and the hardships. Every time.

I had looked too long through the eyes of loss, and I needed to learn how to see differently. The head will follow the heart anywhere. To live with a certainty that God is watching over you, and to move in the world with that confidence, is to believe in both God and oneself. This is what I really came to Sinai to learn. This is where I would find that missing God of mine, in the heart of my own trust. But I didn't know that yet.

Now might be a good time to talk about God, in general. Or, more precisely, Gods. The God of Christianity, the God of Islam and the God of Judaism are *all the same guy.* One God: God. By whichever faith you call Him.

This God differs in name (The Holy Trinity, Allah, Yahweh), and rituals (baptism, fasting, keeping kosher) and celebrations (Christmas, Ramadan, Yom Kippur). He also differs by virtue of the various individuals who brought His word to mankind (Jesus, Muhammad, Moses), enlightened, charismatic, and inspired by the one God.

Where Judaism stopped at the *Torah*, Christianity picked up with the crucifixion and the *New Testament*. Islam teaches that the story continues, that God sent another prophet, who gave us *Al-Qur'an*.

In the illustrious evolution of faith, Moses lays claim to the Burning Bush (the voice of God), the Ten Commandments and the notion that he and his people are God's chosen ones. ("The Lord your God has chosen you to be a people for Himself, a special treasure above all the peoples on the face of the earth." Deuteronomy 14:2). Jesus is the only one in the pack (in all of history, actually) since Osiris of ancient Egypt, to die, bone dead, and actually spring back to life. ("But now Christ is risen from the dead, the first fruits of them that sleep." I Corinthians 15:20). Muhammad enjoys the distinction of being last. Which is a good deal for him. Muhammad had the foresight to declare, in advance, that he would be the very last in this inspired string of holy messengers. ("Muhammad is not the father of any of your men, but he is the Apostle of Allah and the Last of the prophets." Shakir XXXIII.040).

For Islam, no more prophets shall follow. None. Another, modern prophet translating God's most recent and critical press releases, would not come along. Not ever.

This might have been the most brilliant marketing strategy since Peter became the rock of the orthodox church and formed an irrefutable hierarchy of religious power. With God at the pinnacle, and layers of popes, bishops and priests in between, the common folk had no other avenue, no other means to reach God. None but through the structure of The Church. Period. Redemption, salvation and life eternal were wholly-owned subsidiaries of organized religion. This hierarchy is the indomitable structure that that raised Christianity from an obscure, marginalized sect of outcasts to the religious and financial powerhouse it is today.

Amr told me pretty much everything I knew about Islam at the time. And he believed it. Fervently. As gently and fervently as I believe that Jesus of Nazareth died on the cross to save me from my sins.

I *am* the teesiest bit skeptical, however, about the resurrection. It seems more likely that this was a metaphorical affair. That Mary Magdalene saw Jesus in a vision and was reborn in her heart and her mind and her soul. As well as the souls of the twelve disciples and the sixty zillion Christians since then. It's hard to build a world religion on a metaphor, though. The resurrection is the sacred cow of Christianity. Without it, you've got. . . well, Judaism.

I wonder, though, if all the propaganda couldn't be distilled to one salient point: one single law of God to live and die by?

Christian: All things whatsoever ye would that men should do to you, do ye even so to them.

Jewish: Whatsoever thou hatest thyself, that do not to another.

Muslim: No one of you is a believer until he desires for his brother that which he desires for himself.

Buddhist: Hurt not others in ways that you would find hurtful.

Confucian: Do not unto others what you would not have them do unto you.

Hindu: This is the sum of duty: do naught unto others which if done to thee would cause thee pain.

Sikh: I am a stranger to no one: and no one is a stranger to me, indeed I'm a friend to all.

Taoist: Regard your neighbor's gain as your own gain, and your neighbor's loss as your own loss.

Zoroastrian: That nature alone is good which refrains from doing unto another whatsoever is not good for itself.

Well, who am I to quibble? I truly do not know.

The leaders of the Inquisition knew, of course. The Crusaders knew. The judges of the Salem witch trials knew. The missionaries running roughshod in the Congo knew. The assassins of the Muslim Brotherhood knew. Arial Sharon knew. The 911 terrorists knew. The White House knew.

To move through life with fanatical certainty must be a relief and a source of comfort. I prefer the kindness of uncertainty.

And there you have it: my simple understanding of comparative religion. It's part of my journey, part of my ongoing quest, to know and to understand God. Abandoned children like me see the world through a different lens: one of being forgotten, of being left behind. The first great abandonment, of course, was being spit out of the ethereal heavens and through the birth canal. Abandoned by God.

I thought I would find Him, and remind Him—there on Sinai—that I was down here and I was struggling. He found me first. I was crying on a beach, in clothes that didn't match, my hair sixteen ways from Sunday, swimming toward hope—the way He created me.

CHAPTER EIGHT

I REMEMBER SINAI

RA: *The sun god, Ra, is worshipped as the creator of everything.*

The minivan left at midnight, with nine of us crammed inside like international sardines. Nine strangers, mismatched and tossed together willy-nilly, with one common interest: to walk God's mountain.

It was going to be a long, miserable ride. I left the coastal paradise of Dahab on a tiny, fold-down seat the size of a dinner plate, into the stark, rugged interior of the peninsula. My compatriots had napped through the evening to prepare for the rigors of the climb ahead. Sitting there, wishing I had a window or a friendly shoulder to lean against, I wondered why I hadn't done the same.

Two hours later, we unscrewed ourselves from the minivan and stood blinking into the dark. We could only see vague outlines of each other shuffling quietly in the night, but there were a billion zillion stars in the sky and we could see them all. Naturally, the girls all had to pee first thing. The lavatory was locked—probably a good thing—because had we seen it in the broad light of day, we might have gotten ourselves straight back on the van to Dahab. A British girl and I found a patch of sand beside a building, and unceremoniously christened it The Ladies Room. I felt guilty squatting there on God's mountain, but Necessity has her demands.

St. Catherine's—the oldest continuously inhabited monastery in the world—served as our base of operations. Located mid-mountain, at 4,900 feet, this bastion has kept the Christian faith for 1,700 straight and holy years. A square fortress, with granite walls rising up 200 feet, the monastery covers the breadth of a city block and houses the smallest diocese in the world: monks preparing for the afterlife by serving God in this one. This isolated stronghold also boasts priceless works of Byzantine art—including icons, mosaics, wall paintings, and miniatures—and one of the largest collections of illuminated writings in the world, second only to the Vatican. Some 3,500 volumes, written in eight different languages, have been catalogued, including a letter of guaranteed protection in the Prophet Muhammad's own hand.

Gardens and cypress trees surround the monastery, but hard dusty scrabble covers the rest of the land, rising toward the jutting edifice of Mount Horeb. The centerpiece of St. Catherine's, its reason for existence, the source of its mystery, and the living artifact that has drawn thousands of pilgrims for hundreds of centuries, is the Burning Bush. The Burning Bush, through which God spoke directly to Moses. If such a thing could really happen, could it happen for me, here in this place, at tomorrow's new light? Could I hear the voice of God? Even if it was just a word? Even if it was just a whisper?

From the monastery, we launched our attack on the 2,600 vertical feet still rising between us and the summit. There, the sun would light upon the very same place on earth where Moses received the Ten Commandments of God. And we would be its witnesses.

But first, the Steps of Repentance. Orthodox monks built 3,750 steep steps into the barren mountainside, adorned with arches and chapels of stone. This path has also been called the Stairway to Heaven. The distinction, I believe, depends on whether you are heading up them, or down.

Most tourists who climb Mount Sinai choose another path, a longer path, gently sloped and winding to the top. Still, a four-hour excursion waited them, in the dark, on an unfamiliar path. It is said that the local Bedouins—with camels for rent—just hang around and wait for people to collapse. I chose the steps.

Our little enclave from Dahab met up with organized tour groups and random travelers and we all milled around waiting for some holy green light or sign from the heavens that it was time to set out. I chatted over a cigarette with two mates from London, Matthew and Humphrey. They'd gone to Sharm el-Sheikh to dive and wound up at St. Catherine's on a lark. I was happy to be hearing simple English. They said they were glad for "sensible company" for a change. Matthew was the silliest of the two, lighthearted, easy going. He had a broad smile, hair cut short and the look of someone with a constant stream of friendly mischief on his mind. Humphrey was the more handsome, more serious, more brilliant. Blonde, tall, confident, he gave me the impression of someone who just dropped out of prep school to travel to the dusty corners of the world. We decided to trek up the steps together.

People were clustering around their guides and climbing onto the backs of uninspired camels. I asked someone where the steps started and a guide shook his head and graciously handed me a flashlight. "That way," he sighed.

Undaunted, Matthew, Humphrey and I charged off in the dark toward the stairs. The trail wasn't marked, so with three flashlights darting against a landscape of gray rock, we sought our path. Bedouins tried to give us directions, but most didn't understand us at all, and when they did, they urged us toward the other path. We would have none of it, and stumbled through the darkness on our own.

We found the way thanks only to Humphrey's logic, a vague trail, and the good grace of God. That and a general sense of which way was upward. I worked hard to keep up with the guys. "I'm so glad I started smoking again when I got to Egypt," I said, between gasps of cold air. "I'm so glad I started smoking when I was 14," replied Matthew.

We listed as many of the Ten Commandments as we could remember, and I silently noted the ones I had broken. "Thou shalt honor thy mother and thy father... Thou shalt remember the Sabbath and keep it holy... Thou shalt not steal..."

If the Steps of Repentance put an ear to my silent confessions that night, they would have heard this: That I hate my parents, as much as I am bound by love to them. To the exact degree that I adored them and put them on cherished pedestals, they in turn dashed and disappointed me. I don't know if I ever really felt their love. Though I know in my head they both loved me deeply.

As for the Sabbath, well, Sundays are tremendously suitable for sleeping in, drinking champagne and making love out of wedlock. Admit it. A lonely Sunday, in a series of lonely Sundays, is also less sacred than the Monday that takes you out of the abyss and back into the land of the living.

I stole lip gloss once, in the seventh grade. I got caught and the whole episode absolutely mortified me. Imagine calling my dad, *my dad*, and asking him to please pick me up at the police station. Truthfully, the shame of that experience stayed with me my whole life. But it was really Suzette Gerz's fault, because she taught me how to steal, by example. She was what my grandmother would call a troublemaker.

"Thou shalt not take the Lord thy God's name in vain …" My list of sins went on.

Then Humphrey, Mathew and I listed the northern states of America— Washington to Wisconsin to Maine—why, I cannot now imagine. It's not as easy as it sounds. And it's funny as hell. Matthew and Humphrey didn't laugh at their own jokes, or each other's, but that made them even funnier. I giggled and gasped all three arduous hours to the top.

I got rest breaks by stopping and pointing out constellations in the sky; Matthew and Humphrey said they'd never seen such stars. I showed them the three-starred belt of Orion, which is aligned perfectly with the three great pyramids of Egypt. We found the North Star, Venus, Cassiopeia and the Big Dipper, which they called the Sauce Pan. The night sky is a familiar friend to me, a great mystery and an awesome spectacle. I cannot imagine not knowing it.

Looking toward the summit, we saw several dots of light sprinkled against the black mountain. Mystified, we pondered the possibilities: Pilgrims with big flashlights? Lampposts? Tent camps? Hearty entrepreneurs manning hot chocolate stands?

Indeed, as we approached the first light we found a little ramshackle hut, lit with a Coleman lantern and furnished with a solitary cot. A cardboard sign announced: water, tea, coffee, hot cocoa, cookies, biscuits and candy bars for sale. A Bedouin, bundled head to toe in heavy layers, shifted his weight to keep warm.

How in the great wide world of free enterprise did a Coleman lantern find its way to a rock mountain on the Sinai Peninsula? Ebay? Not likely. Regardless, we three weary travelers bellied up to the counter and ordered our mid-mountain snack. My mates bought hot chocolate and "chockie bars," Snickers to be precise. This sent me over the top. But if a Coleman lantern could find its way to Sinai, why not a box of Snickers? I wondered, though, did they come straight from the factory in Nevada? Or did they come in bulk from Costco? Was there a vast Bedouin distribution network staged in Suez? My great spiritual quest spiraled into the considerations of more practical matters. How exactly does one set up shop on the mountain of Moses to sell coffee and cookies at 6,000 feet?

The solitary proprietor didn't speak English. But he took our American dollars and Egyptian pounds and hopefully considered it a good night's work. I would never unravel the mystery of him. And the sun would not wait for me. A Cadbury bar, bad coffee and a few minutes of rest, and I joined Matthew and Humphrey on our final passage to the top.

People such as me, whose dreams are bigger than our capabilities, become intimate with disappointment. We become accustomed to striving. We search endlessly for thin golden threads in the complicated tapestry that makes up our lives.

Which is why, when Humphrey announced, "That rock looks like a face," my heart did a layout-back-handspring. About three-quarters of the way up the steps, we had stopped for another breather and some water. I concerned myself with the temperature—which was falling rapidly—and wrapped myself in the one thin sweater I'd brought. But when Humphrey said, "Look," I forgot the cold and the sweat and the toil.

A huge, serious profile jutted out from the mountainside, gazing across the vast, low land: brow, eyes, nose, lips, chin. I had expected more of a vision or an epiphany. I rose and laid my hand on the cool stone. Where are you, God, if not here—if not in my heart and my efforts and in this good company? *Where are you?*

We were quiet now, the three of us following our own thoughts on the cold hard mountain, wherever they wanted to take us.

The temperature plummeted as we continued upward. The combination of exertion and anticipation kept me warm, but it wasn't to last. Very near the top we stopped and spoke to a young couple hunkered down, smoking pot in a nook behind some rocks. They had been to the mountaintop, declared it absurdly cold, and retreated for better comforts.

Just below the summit we stopped at another Bedouin shack, where they rented wool blankets and thin mattress pads, cheap: at five pounds apiece. That would be the best $1.47 I spent the entire trip. I was woefully underdressed. I hadn't pictured Moses in a Patagonia, fleece-lined, thermal-tested parka with ventilation zippers. If Moses could walk to the top of Mount Sinai in nothing more than a striped moo-moo, well then by God, I could do it in a t-shirt and a thin sweater.

I had things to learn on Sinai.

The summit boasts a slightly-less-than-balmy 40 degrees Fahrenheit. In Montana parlance: butt-ass-cold. Shivering violently, I could honestly report that I was colder than I had ever been or thought I could be. *Ever.*

I wondered in passing when my two blankets had last been laundered, if ever, but didn't linger on the point. Some things are better left alone. I wrapped them around my shoulders and shuffled my way up the final path. It was three o'clock in the morning.

Sunrise wouldn't come for two more hours. Matthew carried my hot cocoa and bedding up the last few, steepest yards of the mountain. We crawled, in the dark, over sharp slabs of rock to the east slope of the summit. With the exception of one ambitious man who had packed up a camera, tri-pod, and fanny pack full of film, we were the only people there.

One giant step from the top, I settled myself onto a flat, smooth ledge, six feet wide and a straight vertical drop to the valley floor below. My perch inclined back into the body of the mountain and I felt totally safe in the arms of Mt. Sinai. I hunkered down in my blankets and fantasized about a warm and cozy nap. It was not to be.

Fifty other travelers joined us before the sun arrived. We waited together in chatter, cigarette smoke and the anticipation of dawn. This was no place for quiet contemplation, mystical transformation, or a life-changing spiritual moment. Still, I closed my eyes from time to time to look for something bigger than me and to breathe away the noise and rattling cold.

Humble, low and lonely, in the dark morning hours, came the sound of chanting. As the music of voices drifted up the mountain, I wondered what life was like for the monks in the land below. I wondered what mysteries they understood, that we travelers passed through and by, and never noticed.

For two solid hours I stared at an ink black void, waiting for daylight. Then the stars began to disappear. Dawn was coming. The sun finally began to bleed slowly into the dark of night at about 5:15 in the morning. While I watched the thin ribbon of light widen in the sky, it seemed as though I could actually feel the earth turning itself, and me with it, slowly to the east.

Another 45 minutes passed before we saw the orb of the sun itself. This magnificent orange-red sphere brought more than light and warmth to us. It brought a sense of accomplishment. Our journeys were validated by the simple, common rising of the sun that, 364 other days that year, didn't matter much to any of us.

The crowd came alive as if the curtain was rising on a great stage. Voices and exclamations rose over a symphony of shutter-clicks. I threw off my blankets, the cold and contemplation forgotten, and moved forward against an outcropping of rocks, jockeying for a good camera angle. At this point, Humphrey—king of the night, fearless leader of our band of three—got nervous. I think he felt that he needed to guide and protect us all.

A very pretty woman from Europe, young and used to attention, started to walk along a narrow ledge. Unless an earthquake suddenly struck or some fool decided to murder her in front of 50 people by giving her a nice firm shove, she was perfectly safe. But not in Humphrey's mind. "Please don't do that," he implored. "Please come back." Her silhouette framed beautifully against the sunrise, she paused, turned and looked at Humphrey like a bug she should squash.

How can a person be so beautiful and so ugly in the same moment? I intervened on Humphrey's behalf with my kill-her-with-kindness, let's-all-get-along strategy. "You should take her picture, Humphrey," I said. "She looks so beautiful."

"You can't take my picture," she replied curtly. "My face is copyrighted."

I thought to say: *You're in the public domain, sister. Anyone can take your picture, any time, anywhere, doing anything, as long as you're in a public place. Like this place, for just one example. And they can do whatever they want with it, including post it on the Internet with the caption: Blonde dies on Sinai. So shut up and smile for Humphrey's camera, you screaming self-absorbed bitch.* But I kept my mouth shut. God's mountain is no place for a catfight.

Humphrey was still nervous about her precarious position next to a deadly 1,000-foot drop, but she wasn't going to be told what to do. I, personally, wasn't worried about her. Her life was probably copyrighted, and neither God nor gravity would claim it. Not yet anyway.

There were no signs saying, DANGER: KEEP AWAY FROM LEDGE, no railing, no ropes, no man-made viewing platforms. Nothing had been put up to make this safe or squeaky-tourist-clean. Or to reduce an owner's risk of liability in case a damn fool tourist slipped and hurt or killed herself. Who would she sue? The Bedouins? The monks? God? We were on our own and expected to look out for ourselves. I liked that. And, with Humphrey's supervision, we did.

As dawn settled in and people began to set aside their cameras, a group of Korean travelers gathered on an outcropping of rock and began to sing. Everyone turned to watch and listen. We asked Humphrey what they were singing, because we knew he would know. "Just wait until they get to the chorus," he said. "You'll recognize it." I stood with my friends in the cold air of morning and heard, in the Korean language, on the top of Mount Sinai, *Amazing Grace*.

Five years ago to the day, the sun had set on Terry's life, even as it rose that morning on Sinai.

There was nothing left to do but climb down the mountain.

What a miserable affair. Crowds jostled along the stairs in a thick unruly fashion. Start. Stop. Start. Stop. Bitch. Moan. Start. Stop. I had to pee, badly. I should have stayed up top alone. But in my haste to find a bathroom, I jostled with the mob instead, down 3,750 stone steps. Thus, I missed my last big chance for a spiritual epiphany. I would carry my burden, whatever sorrows or demons I'd brought up there, back down the mountain with me.

Add to this the mistake of buying rocks at the top. Indeed: rocks. The Bedouins sell stones from the mountain, about the size of eggs, as souvenirs. Each one is broken into two pieces, dull and rough on the outside, but embedded with magnificent crystals. Two halves of a whole, soul mates, split-aparts, like Terry and me.

It's in my nature to contemplate rocks and sunrises and people. To scrape at the surface of things. If a rock, broken in half, could reveal beauty, couldn't it reveal wisdom? Couldn't it whisper into my ear: *Beautiful and ugly co-exist in the same spaces, in the same moments. Bad things happen to good people. Life is more than it appears. Grief is lovely. Grace is everywhere.* Couldn't it tell me that somewhere, broken into pieces, there was something beautiful inside of me?

I thought of the grapevines growing in the rocky soil of Burgundy, France. Too sweet the soil, and the grapes become a plain and simple fruit. It's the struggle that gives them their complexity; the journey gives them their character. Wasn't the same true for me? Or was I just a dreamer, who purchased her rocks at the top?

Never mind that 20 little children were waiting at St. Catherine's to sell those same rocks. That hadn't occurred to me. No. I have the get-it-while-you-can-before-the-going-gets-gone philosophy. Wouldn't want to lose out on two pounds of rocks to carry on my back down a steep hill for 2,600 feet. Maybe I didn't want to let go of my burden, my sorrow, my loss. Maybe I wanted to pile it on, like the guilt and the regrets. Everything dreamy and possible in the night seemed harsh and unyielding in the glaring light of day.

Naturally, everyone wanted to take the steps down the mountain instead of the camel path. Nobody told them that going down was actually *harder* in many ways than going up. Middle-aged, out-of-shape tour-bus types hollered at each other, complained and gasped and fell repeatedly all the way to St. Catherine's. In better circumstances, I might have thought it sweet how they tried and struggled, and helped each other along. But all I could see was my own need for a bathroom, a crowded path, and garbage all over the steps.

A woman in front of me pulled a bright blue wad of yarn from her pocket and dropped it—as if she had no brain—right on the steps. I picked it up and carried it another ten yards down the Steps of Frustration to a garbage can.

I was coming to regard the tourists on Mount Sinai as rude, loud, arrogant, litterbugs. Plastic cups, empty cigarette packs, candy bar wrappers and all manner of cast-offs lay strewn across the mountain. Those and about a billion cigarette butts. Forget that there were trash receptacles all along the way. Why carry your junk 50 feet when you can just drop it on the ground? God will clean up after you.

Hot, tired, thirsty and hungry, I finally made it to the bottom and bee-lined it to a water closet. For a second I thought I'd stepped into Hell. The lavatory was filthy, not more than a hole in the floor, without the hot running water I longed for, without *toilet paper*. I'd roughed it before, plenty, in the wilderness. But this was something else altogether. I had expectations. I had *needs*. Sanitary facilities ought to be a requirement, I thought. When Amr described Sinai as "rustic," I never imagined dirty toilets. Couldn't he have just said, "Kyla, whatever happens, take your own toilet paper"?

I decided to walk down the long dusty road to the main gate. Maybe there would be a bathroom there. I caught up with a guide who I recognized from the mountain. His customers had stopped, gasping and griping, on the way down. Passing by them, I had fallen on the narrow steps. The guide had vigorously rubbed grit from the scrapes in my hands. He told me I was beautiful and asked my name and my country. Then he invited me to breakfast with his patrons.

"Yes, you will come," he said. "It's only five minutes from here. We'll drive. Come to breakfast with us." Surely a restaurant would have hot running water, and I was really hungry, but I had to meet my driver in another hour. Besides, nothing was as easy as it sounded on Sinai. The quick breakfast, five minutes away, would probably turn into a three-hour escapade. Wandering away from my one chance to get back to Cairo on time didn't seem prudent.

"No thanks," I said. "I can't. But do you know where there's a bathroom?"

"You can't go to breakfast?"

"No, seriously. But I really need a bathroom."

"Oh well, there's a bathroom down here. Very nice." He pointed to the main gate and we walked together and talked while he left his customers to trail behind in the rising dust.

Camel drivers scour this long road calling to travelers with rides for sale. More children walk in the heat and dirt with egg-shaped stones in shallow, cardboard boxes. I wondered in passing if those were the boxes the Snickers came in.

The "very nice" bathroom at the main gate was as gross as anything I'd ever seen. *And* a man followed me through the open door with a mop that looked like a windshield wiper on a stick. Whatever he did with that thing all the live-long day couldn't possibly be worth whatever tips he earned. I shooed him away, let loose my bladder, and walked back to the monastery.

By now, my mood had deteriorated to crankiness. I reached in my pocket for my Chapstick. *It was gone.* I had no Chapstick! Of all the discomforts on Sinai, this was the worst. Let me admit it right now: I'm a long-time, non-recovering, self-confessed Chapstick addict. I thought I might just lose my mind on the spot. But then I remembered that I had lipstick in my backpack. All morning long, I lubed up my lips in the dry heat with Lancôme's Nude 2 Lip Perfecting Pencil.

I'm addicted to Chapstick. I admit it. I love Chapstick. I never leave home without it. I carry a tube of the waxy drug in my pocket, every waking hour of every single day. Even my pajama pants have pockets. Chapstick on the left; Kleenex on the right. I'm a creature of habit.

You don't want to be around me if I lose my Chapstick. In the water, say, because I was wakeboarding with it—yes, even my swimwear has pockets—and when I went down, the Chapstick went down. Down, down, down to the bottom of the lake, never to be seen again. Poor, sad Chapstick.

Someone once told me that Chapstick was manufactured with tiny, little bitty micro-chards of glass, and even as the waxy product soothes your lips, it simultaneously damages them. So you always need more and more and more. I don't care. Chapstick won't be the first object of my desire that injured me.

My dad, it turns out, was a Chapstick addict, too, from way back in the day when Chapstick tubes were made out of real tin. I can still see him withdrawing the black-andwhite dispenser from his pocket, as natural and easy as breathing.

This is his legacy to me, I suppose: A wild attraction to Chapstick, and the ability to soothe and damage in the same deft stroke.

So there I sat, wearing pink lipstick, wondering where the priests went to the bathroom. Surely they had a real toilet and a sink. I couldn't imagine a priest squatting over a hole in the ground without toilet paper and no opportunity to wash his hands. I wondered, too, about the Bedouin and their children. Where did they live? How did they bathe? What did they eat? I've moved through so many moments in life, untouched, unaware, self-absorbed. Sinai would not let me.

So I slogged along with a blister on my toe, in clothes I'd worn for four days, with my hair sticking out in all directions, and killed time with the locals until the monastery opened. I plopped down a stone ledge, drank a Pepsi, and let myself be accosted by children selling rocks. I took their pictures and let them take mine. I learned their names. I didn't need two more pounds of rocks on my back, but I gave them all money anyway. This was their life. No Nintendo or Game Boy, only selling. I couldn't guess where their mothers were.

I took a picture of a fuzzy-faced camel, offering *baksheesh* to its owner and wishing I could pet the animal like a puppy. He looked sweet enough, and underappreciated, with red tassels hanging from his head. But several people had told me that camels spit. Yes, they curl up their lips and pepper unsuspecting tourists with saliva. Just what I needed. So I moved on. The time had come to see the Burning Bush, snap a few pictures and catch my ride to Cairo.

The Burning Bush—the very one through which God spoke to Moses— grows in the courtyard of St. Catherine's. They say people have tried to transplant sprigs of it, but it won't grow anywhere else in the world. In the crowded monastery I made my way to a small garden court, past a big hanging vine and straight into Matthew and Humphrey.

"Hello!"

A man shooed me out of the way. I was obstructing some big photo opp. *So sorry.* I moved aside and asked my mates, "So... have you seen the bush yet?"

"Right there." Matthew pointed behind me.

I spun around. *"That's* the Burning Bush?" The bush grew up behind a tall lattice and fell above our heads in a thousand tendrils of vine. I had somehow pictured a charred twig-looking thing. But of course, it was the Burning Bush, not the Burnt Bush. Photo Man was underneath, yanking and twisting on a vine to take away with him. It wouldn't break off. He had to settle for the mangled leaves he raked off with his hand, his piece of God.

All of the vines within reach had been stripped bare. The leaves above grew green and lush, but only tiny, new buds could be found isolated here and there on the ends. It would not be long before these, too, would be shredded off. The courageous buds that would replace them, tenaciously unfolding, reaching towards life, wouldn't have a prayer. I touched a doomed bud gently with my finger. I was sick to death of tourists.

I wanted to get off Sinai and back to my clean, friendly hotel in Cairo. But of course, the more you long for something, the more it eludes you.

In Dahab, Salém had arranged for me to meet "someone" at 10 A.M. at the monastery for my ride back to Cairo that day. I couldn't miss that ride. A plane would leave from Cairo for Luxor the next morning and I had to be on it. Negotiations with Salém included much eager head-nodding—*yes, yes, no problem*—and whispers to colleagues in Arabic. My part was to hand over the cash. No ticket, no receipt, no brochure. Just blind faith. In America we're more organized. We're licensed. We have set schedules printed on slick paper. A person knows, generally, what to expect. None of this was true in Egypt.

My driver would find me, Salém had promised. So I milled around, waiting impatiently, eating a package of crackers. When a man in a *jaballiyah* approached me, I shrugged him off, not in the mood to be sold a camel ride, a taxi, a postcard, a rock. "From America," he pressed, gesturing to me. "Ride to Cairo." Oops. He explained that I would be going with four others to Cairo and pointed to a van.

Then he said something in Arabic and held out his hand. "No, I paid Salém," I insisted. "I paid Salém, in full, in Dahab!" He kept repeating his request. "No, no," I said, causing a rather big scene. Someone stepped forward and said, "It's okay. Don't worry." He spoke to the man in Arabic and then turned to me. "You have his flashlight?"

"Oh, sorry." I didn't recognize the man who had thought to look after me the night before by loaning me a flashlight. I'd suddenly become as obnoxious as the tourists I had criticized. I had spiraled into Schmuckville and I couldn't get out. Not until I had a hot soapy shower.

I found Matthew and gave him a warm hug him goodbye. His fine company and good humor made a lasting impression on me. I could see his heart just beyond his smile, not hidden like in most people. Humphrey was off buying postcards. I would miss them both, but they had other destinations.

Four travelers from the Philippines eventually gathered themselves together and joined me for the long drive to Cairo. I climbed into the front seat of the van and dared to check my look in the mirror. I was a disaster. And I had lipstick on my teeth.

The van driver, as cranky and confused as anyone, spent the next hour trying to get us out of the neighborhood. He drove around asking questions and trying to get the proper authorization to transport us to Cairo. When most people leave for a trip, they get in the car and go. Not so on Sinai. We wasted the first half hour going nowhere. We eventually found ourselves at the office of the Tourist Police, where we had to show our passports and put our names on some arbitrary list. Then we went back to the monastery for more signatures and more waiting. Finally, Judy, a Philippine who worked as a nurse in a military hospital in Saudi Arabia, and actually spoke some Arabic, got out to hustle things along. She actually helped. With stupendous relief, we finally left the gates of St. Catherine's for Cairo.

I wondered what heartbreaks, addictions, disappointments and failures each one of us might have come to leave behind on Mount Sinai. What I left behind was a little, lost tube of Chapstick beside a rock somewhere. That and many expectations.

It would be seven long, hot, aggravating hours before I finally walked back into the Nile Hilton that night. We stopped frequently at checkpoints along the way, where armed police strolled solemnly through the van, scrutinizing us and our passports. I wondered what wily quirk or suspicious characteristic might alarm them, causing them to haul a person off the van for . . . what? Questioning? Interrogation? A mysterious disappearance in the desert? We'd sit like helpless little bugs under a magnifying glass and wait for them to hand back the little blue books that legitimized our existence. Even more disturbing: our driver would just up and disappear every chance he got, returning 20 minutes later without a word or glance. To me, he represented yet another mystery on Sinai that I would never understand.

I did come to understand one thing about Sinai: the heat. Miles and miles of it ran in every direction. A strip of highway cuts through the yawning desert, dotted with lonely checkpoints. At each one, four or five men stand around a shack, wearing black wool (wool!) uniforms and smoking cigarettes. It's a wonder they don't all die from heat prostration, cancer or sheer boredom. Egypt seems filled with monotonous jobs like these, perfect Petri dishes for breeding resentment, civil unrest and solidarity. They say poverty breeds terrorism—poverty and hopelessness. But how does that account for Osama bin Laden, born into wealth and rage?

These are the thoughts that occupy the mind in the middle of the desert, where everything seems endless and dry and forlorn; where there are no boundaries to rein in the imagination.

By now, I couldn't get out of Sinai fast enough.

Between Sinai and Cairo we crossed the Suez Canal—one of the most significant stretches of water on the planet. This shipping zone crosses 101 miles, linking the Mediterranean (at Port Said) with the Red Sea (at Suez). As early as 1869, its waters provided a trade route between Europe and Asia. It also made the penetration and colonization of Africa exponentially more enticing to the Europeans. Today, war ships, aircraft carriers and cargo vessels, carrying everything from crude oil to cashmere, pay tolls for passage, supplying Egypt with a hefty source of revenue.

Not everyone has always been happy about Egypt's control of the canal, however. Geography—completely arbitrary, completely indifferent to the plights of humankind—inevitably becomes the hinge pin to war and commerce. So, when Egyptian President Nasser nationalized the canal in 1956 to help fund the building of the great dam at Aswan, Britain, France and Israel pitched a fit and invaded Egypt. Egypt responded by sinking the 40 ships that happened to be in the canal at the time. When the Soviet Union threatened to intervene on Egypt's behalf, the United States and Canada joined the fray and helped negotiate peace.

With its enormous impact on international trade, the canal became Egypt's political trump card and played a pivotal role in mid-eastern conflicts through the decades.

In 1967, angry that the canal had been closed to them since 1949, Israel launched a no-holes-barred preemptive strike against Egypt. It didn't help that Egypt had amassed 1,000 tanks and 100,000 soldiers at Israel's southern border. Syria and Jordon joined Egypt in the aptly named Six-Day War. The conflict lasted 132 hours and 30 minutes and the Arabs got their butts kicked. They lost the Gaza Strip, Sinai, East Jerusalem, Jordon's West Bank, and Syria's Golan Heights.

Egypt closed the canal for eight years. Forced to circumnavigate Africa or portage across land, ships incurred enormous costs in time and fuel. Egypt's blockade also trapped 14 vessels, known as the Yellow Fleet, in the bright blue waters of the Great Bitter Lake. In this southern section of the canal, desert sand accumulated onboard the abandoned ships for almost a decade, giving rise to the fleet's lonely, haunting nickname.

The canal re-opened in 1975 and a peace agreement between Egypt and Israel allowed Israel unrestricted use. In 1981, the Multinational Force and Observers—under agreements between Egypt, Israel and the United States—set up camp in Sinai to phase Israel out of the Sinai peninsula and enforce the Egypt-Israel Peace Treaty of 1979. Thus the shipping canal has enjoyed a quiet truce for nearly three whole decades. Today, 20,000 ships and $2 billion dollars flow through these waters annually, making Suez the busiest canal in the world.

For all the conflicts strewn along this slim blue ribbon of water, the canal itself has no borders, no bindings, no locks. Both ends lay at sea level: a happy, perfectly balanced little pond of global transportation. Only humans carry the walls of war and torment.

In Suez we got another driver—younger, unhappier and more confused than the last. We all piled out of the van as a cluster of men gathered 'round and started barking instructions, all taking and pointing at once. One man finally asked us our destination, in English, and then told the driver what to do in Arabic. Surprise: you have a vanload of people going to Cairo.

The driver then demanded money from us, which sent me right over the edge. The Philippine travelers handed over 100 pounds a piece, but I flat-out refused. Arab men don't seem to care for angry women. But I dug in and restated my claim over and over, adding more volume each time: "I paid Salém in Dahab for my trip—all the way to Cairo!"

"Okay! No money!" The man barked into my face.

"Okay!" Pissed, weary, low on blood sugar and dirty head-to-toe, I slogged myself back into the van. *Would I ever get to Cairo?* I started obsessing about a long, hot, soapy shower and I don't remember thinking of anything else the rest of the way. Until we got lost again.

The driver meandered through downtown Cairo, clearly confused. Finally he just stopped at a vacant parking lot in the pitch dark—I had no idea where—and stated: "You get out here."

A crowd converged on us as we all stepped out of the van, everyone shouting, pointing and shouting back. Surveying this all-too-familiar scene, I wondered why Egyptians seemed to gravitate toward each other, while in America we tend to keep our distance from trouble on the street.

Surprisingly, I was right in the thick of it. "You're not dropping us off in the middle of a parking lot!" I yelled. That much I knew. I didn't know, however, where this voice was coming from. Mine isn't a voice raised to be heard. Mine is a rambling voice, a fast and frenetic voice. A voice interrupted. One that runs from confrontation. But there I was, hollering at an Egyptian van driver. "You are taking us to the Nile Hilton. *Nil Hilton!*"

"Don't worry." A calm and gentle voice emerged from the pack. A young man asked me where I wanted to go.

"The Nile Hilton," I repeated. He translated for the driver and gave him very specific directions, over and over, gesturing with his arms.

"*Shokran, shorkran*," I said. "Thank you very much." We all clambered back into the van and drove away from the quiet voice in the dark as the crowd dissipated into the night.

I nearly wept with relief in the elegant bathroom of the Nile Hilton that night. A flushing commode. Hot running water. Miles of toilet paper. I looked like an apparition in the mirror. What I saw, though, as I washed the dirt from my hands and face, was the promise travel had kept.

A trace of Sinai lingers still, and calls to me here in America, in a life embraced by the familiar and the ordinary. It is saying, if I will listen, *You. You there. Pay attention. You are more than this. Remember. Remember. . .* And I remember Sinai.

Chapter Nine

The Love Boat of the Nile

ISIS: *As the wife of Osiris and mother of Horus, Isis epitomizes feminine qualities. She possesses great magical powers and, as the goddess of two worlds, invokes the powers of both heaven and earth.*

I slid through five days and nights on The Nile Romance with nothing more to worry about than when the next tour left and what flavor of wine I was going to drink that day. I lived in a motorized Shambala. I did, however, have a miserable head cold, chest congestion, two big blisters on my big toe, screaming calves, a toothache, my period, and goofy hair. I also came down with a screaming case of acute homesickness.

My one sure-fire cure for homesickness is to focus, is to pay attention to something or someone other than myself. Like other people, for example, their prides and plights; like art and architecture; like 6,000-year-old paint. Alone, in the dark, in the bewitching hours between night and day, however, that's impossible.

Tuesday / November 16 / Luxor

Three o'clock in the morning came way too early. I hung up the phone from the wakeup call at the Grand Hotel and fell instantly back to sleep. I knew perfectly well that I had to catch a 6 A.M. flight to Luxor. But I was just so damn tired. And sleep has a mind of its own. What was shaping up to be a missed flight and general travel disaster was short-circuited 15 minutes later. Breakfast was delivered to my room at 3:15 on the dot, with a loud, repeated banging on my door. My throat hurt, it was dark, I was naked and I couldn't find the light. But I was up, by God. I think I drank my lime juice in two seconds flat. The warm croissant tasted good, but anything else, like jam for example, was far too complicated to manage.

I stumbled around the room thick and slow: brush my teeth, wash my face, do something with my hair, my feet hurt, where's that safety pin?, don't forget anything, don't be late, check out, find a taxi. My mind was nothing more that a list and a longing for rest.

When I was ready, I slogged my 50-pound suitcase and backpack to the elevator. The hotel would keep my suitcase in storage until I returned. My backpack was all that would go with me. *Ring. Ring. Ring ring ring ring ring!* I couldn't make the damn elevator work. After one flight of lugging my crap down the stairs, I tried again. *Ring.* The lift began its indifferent, well-slept way up to me. I looked down the hollow elevator shaft seven flights, and when the lift lurched to a stop at my floor, I saw my pale, unhappy face reflected in its mirrors.

The taxi driver on the street wanted 25 pounds for a trip to the airport. And he had a pal conveniently standing by his cab, assuring me that the rate was fair. It just pissed me off. "Ten pounds," I countered.

"No, no," he replied. "To the airport: 25 pounds."

I tried once more: "Fifteen pounds?" His answer: No. 25 pounds. I turned to face the street and hailed another taxi.

The next guy had a better offer: "Twenty pounds to the airport." Forget it, Pal. I'd had about three hours of sleep in three days, much of which was comprised of dirt and hell, and every muscle in my body hurt. Buzz off.

My third effort landed me a junk heap of a taxi for 15 pounds.

Now might be a good time to talk about bargaining. The all-time bargaining champion of the planet in the solar system of The Child Kyla was, bar none, my grandmother. She was in fact, the sun around which all of us orbited.

Will you take a nickel? This was at a rummage sale. Any one of the zillion rummage sales to which I accompanied her. I was mortified. The object, whatever is was—a candle, a knickknack, a vase, a skein of yarn—was originally priced at a *dime*. She got her price, though. She knew what second-hand yarn was worth.

Gramma grew up in the Great Depression. She raised four children on her own. Her first husband had this teensy little mean streak, which was exacerbated by his great big drinking problem. She divorced him and opened a café in eastern Montana, called Aunt Effie's. She sewed her children's clothes and knitted their mittens. When she sold the restaurant, and moved to Missoula to marry my future Grampa, she kept the plates. They were thick and white and they had thin green stripes on the rim. And those were the same plates that we ate off in our cabin in the woods, by Ashby Creek, where we stored up happy memories like nickels in a jar.

I could have used her in Cairo. Gramma would not have been duped by enterprising cab drivers. She might have been suckered in by the little kids, though. She might, in fact, have been the only person to buy more bookmarkers in Egypt than I did. But she would have insisted that they comb their hair and wash under their fingernails. Even if she had to buy them the soap. She loved children. She was everybody's "Gramma." Her house was the most fun and interesting house on the block.

Effie Morris never traveled far from her home in Montana, other than occasional trips to Seattle, Los Angeles and Tucson, where her adult children had migrated. Except to the cabin, always to the cabin. We called the place Camp Gramma. She loved it there, 30 miles outside of Missoula. She adored it; she cherished it.

She hauled up an old firecracker shack and plopped it down on someone else's land by a creek near an aspen tree. My Grampa put windows in it, built bunk beds inside, and the first evolution of Camp Gramma was born. They added to it later, doubled its size, put in a sink and cabinets, a kitchen table with folding leafs, real beds, and a potbelly stove. That's how it became a "real" cabin.

Today, it's a derelict old shack. The bridges we built are feeble and thin. The banks of the creek are overgrown with willows, inaccessible. The potato patch is all weed and dust. No one goes there.

But I travel to that cabin to this day, in my memories, to fish in the stream, fry potatoes in the big, cast iron skillet on the outside stove, and swing over the creek on the Tarzan Ropes. It was a wonderful, magical place. It's gone now, like Gramma and Grampa. Some things you can't get back. Some things you can't bargain for, no matter how many nickels you have.

I arrived at Terminal Three safe and on time, and vastly relieved. I gave the driver a 20-pound note, disinterested in asking for change. Proud of myself for being on time, I promptly spent a half an hour in the wrong line. Nothing was easy.

Wednesday / November 17 / Valley of the Kings

From the Luxor airport, I arrived at The Nile Romance—after some confusion on the part of my taxi driver—much too early to actually check into my cabin. The man at Registration was kind, and patient, and efficient at handling a lone, inconvenient and early guest. My room would be ready in two hours, he said, and in the mean time, I could get some juice at the bar upstairs. Two new friends later, I walked to the sundeck and began writing in my journal.

I was demonstrating to God, day by day, that I could be a travel writer. I was a writer on assignment without an assignment. This wasn't two weeks on the beach in Mexico drinking margaritas and turning my body over every 20 minutes to even my tan. *No sir.* I was looking at everything microscopically, analyzing it, and writing it down before it trundled off into the foggy winds of memory.

I was saying, "See, God, I am worthy to this task. I can travel and write and throw my future baby in a backpack and follow my dreams to the four corners of the earth. And oh, by the way, could you please send me a handsome man to marry and travel the world with, *manfadlak* (please)? ... And also some interesting people to pal around with on this boat. Please don't let them all be German…"

One page of words and I promptly fell asleep.

Sabre woke me when my room was ready and delivery of my luggage had been arranged. Sabre was a guide, hired by the tour company to take people through the various monuments. He was a highly educated babysitter, of sorts. Lunch was to be served a one o'clock and I made myself at home in my tidy little cabin, sweet and clean and on the upper deck. I unpacked, organized, and wrote, happy to be in one place for five whole days.

At lunchtime I was led to The Bales Table, where there was one vacant seat waiting for me. The "Bales Group" was on tour from Devonshire, England, on holiday from their retirement. They welcomed me very warmly to their private enclave, which I thought was very gracious, indeed. Not every one appreciates a "change in plans." But there I was, and I adored them.

They taught me new uses of words, for one thing. "Lovely," for example, has become part of my permanent personal vernacular. I also now employ phrases like "shall we?" and "not at all." Which I learned from these Brits, who seemed to have a leg up on good manners and propriety, compared with us more vulgar Americans. "Don't they?"

There were dozens of such groups aboard the ship, all eating at their own tables, setting out on daily tours together, and generally keeping amongst themselves. Each group had their own hometown leader and their own Egyptian guide to show them the monuments. These guides planned our days, bought our tickets, and tipped the intermediaries.

The fog of uncertainty was beginning to clear: we were Pod People, organized and tended to in the teensiest detail. Counting everyone, we were from Spain, India, Britain, France and America. With the exception of me and one other person, we were over 50.

My first acquaintances were Jean and Joyce from the Bales Group. Jean was a 70-year-old bleach blonde of a buxom woman who had a heart of gold and loved to shop. Her husband died a year prior, and she went to Egypt alone. She would have celebrated her golden anniversary that August. I could see visible traces of loss and loneliness on her face. For one split second, it was like looking in a mirror. She told me her husband had been an engineer for an oil company and they had traveled "quite a bit" in their life together. He was fun, she said, and they had three children and when she looks back at her life, she sees nothing left undone.

Joyce was a sourpuss who kept largely to herself. A permanent frown was etched on her face, even when she was happy about something. I told her I made a friend of the bartender, Mustafa. "He's after your money," she replied. I didn't believe her, and I was sorry for a life that had been so harsh or so disappointing, to have carved permanent unhappiness into a woman.

Roy, our leader, must have been 70. He was gracious, well-traveled, loved Egypt and was a little tiny bit snobby. He was very interested in my novel and what I might write about Egypt in a travel journal. What could I possibly know about *his* Egypt in only two weeks? he wondered. He listed some British bestsellers (*The Grand Piano Came by Camel*, by Christopher Lee, and something else by someone named Freya Star, which doesn't exist, but perhaps I misunderstood), and told me incidents in Aswan recently that related the *real* story of the Egyptian people. My beautiful balloon deflated. I longed for the depth of his knowledge and the life he had had of great adventure.

I didn't know, for example, that if the dam at Aswan ever broke—which holds back the tremendous force of Lake Nasser—the entire country would be wading through a three-mile-high cubic wall of water, from one boarder to the next. Figuratively speaking, of course. But it's a lot of damn dam water.

Yvonne was the sweetest of us all, with a little-girl voice to match. She'd come all that way with great enthusiasm and expectation and spent the first whole day and a half "doing poorly" in her cabin. I loaned her the prettiest and most exquisitely illustrated of my three guidebooks, *Knopf Guides: Egypt*. She seemed surprised that a person would do such a thing.

Pauline and her husband—whose name I can't remember and whose voice I seldom heard—had been married forever and knew each other since they were ten years old. They loved each other's company and took early retirement to "go out a lot" together. They held hands, and she seemed to speak for both of them, as one.

Evelyn and Joe were by far the most charming. Seventy or 80, they held hands, too, and Joe always stuck by Evelyn's side and helped her through the hard steps. Once he left her behind thinking she was foregoing a quick little jaunt to see mummified alligators. She wasn't passing on that activity, though. "Oh, I'll try to catch him," she said, walking slowly, as fast as she could. "Lovie! Lovie, I'm coming!" I wanted to kiss her on the silky soft folds of her face.

Then there was Rosalind, traveling with her son, Alan. Rosalind was gregarious and chatty and fun. She ended every phrase with a disclaimer: ". . . doesn't it?" ". . . aren't they?" ". . . shouldn't we?" She had boatloads of stories and opinions and was ragingly fun to be around.

Lastly, I come to Jill. Her name was really Mary Gwendolyn, but her mother had called her Jill since baby time. This same mother had had a difficult birth with Mary Gwendolyn and would have no more children. She did have an older son, though, named—I swear it's true—Jack. Jill was 80-some years old. The mother and the brother who defined her, were long gone. Jill was also extremely bright, charming, as sharp as a tack and happily active. She noticed everything. She'd been all over the planet and said she, "mostly appreciates the people." She talked and talked and had a lifetime of stories to tell. She drove Joyce crazy, who called her "the old woman," though Joyce herself was 60-something going on 100.

Jill had had some medical problems, she explained, and lived "quite all alone." I knew she had no one to talk to most of the time and I wanted to take her back home to Oregon with me, to be my surrogate grandmother. I wanted her to tell me stories, and ramble, and worry about me, and notice things, as my grandmother did before Alzheimer's took her from us.

That first day in Luxor, there was a field trip to be had. The Valley of the Kings is directly across the Nile to the west of Luxor and just north of the politically less dazzling Valley of the Queens. It's the largest necropolis in Egypt, and gateway for nearly every pharaoh from the New Kingdom into the Afterlife. This includes King Tut, whose empty tomb was—dare I say it?—boring as hell. What was not boring, to me, however, was paint. There was paint on temple walls throughout this valley, paint on towering columns, paint in yellow, red and blue that had been there for 6,000 years. If I had any talent for architecture whatsoever, I'd recreate an Egyptian temple out of matchsticks and glue and gold ... and paint. My God, those temples must have been stunning places.

The air was dry and thick in the valley. Heat radiated in billowing sheets from the sand. The highest peak, *El-Qurn*, loomed powerful and ominous over the necropolis, like the symbolic pyramid of a thousand dead kings. This is a place of death and renewal. Generations of ancient pharaohs are sprinkled in tombs beneath the dry land—buried, lost, mostly forgotten. Thousands of years of sand have blown through this valley, obscuring every human thing underneath ever-increasing layers of new earth.

Hatshepsut's Temple dominated the landscape as our tour bus rounded the last series of sand dunes into the bottom of the valley. This grand monument rises from the desert plain—part mountain, part architecture—as it merges with the sheer cliffs of the Theban Mountain behind it. Built when Egypt was at the peak of its military power, in the 18 dynasty, Hatshepsut dedicated this temple to her father, Tuthmosis I. The massive funerary complex has two levels of columned buildings (Roman-style before Rome existed), separated by three once-lavish terraces. A wide ramp slopes from the sandy ground to the highest terrace.

As I passed the lower terrace to the second colonnade, I could see delicate reliefs and exquisite carvings that told the stories of Hatshepsut's reign: her "divine" birth, her coronation, her life. The ancient colors of red and yellow and blue, though fading, still hinted at a time of glory and pageantry and extraordinary wealth. Virtually every image of the woman king, however, had been scraped from the temple 2,500 years ago, picked away by a mason's tools, and obliterated. Hatshepsut had made her nephew, Tuthmosis III, wait 20 years to ascend the throne of Egypt, and he insisted on his revenge—wiping her from memory.

Hatshepsut rose to power amid a screaming catfight with Tuthmosis III. Following the death of her father, Hatshepsut fought with her younger rival in a bitter and vengeful clash over the right to the throne. The formidable Hatshepsut eventually won the struggle and declared herself Pharaoh. She was the first woman ever in the history of Egypt to rule as *king*. She ruled for 20 years, and for Egypt it was a time of peace and prosperity. No one knows for sure how she died—whether by natural causes or at the hands of her enemies.

Hatshepsut, woman king, took what belonged to her, because she could do it better. Similar to the first woman pharaoh was the last woman pharaoh: Cleopatra. Emil Ludwig wrote this about Cleopatra, "What she did was right because she did it." This made me think that boldness and arrogance have their place. Like walking across a busy street with no stoplight. Like walking into the unknown. Pushing faith into confidence, test driving it at 110 miles per hour on the Autobahn, until you finally own it, and it becomes completely yours.

I wondered what I could accomplish if I were as bold as these Egyptian women, if I didn't always wait to be offered what I wanted.

Tourists flock to Hatshepsut's temple, one of the most stunning monuments of ancient Egypt. On this particular day, a wreath of white flowers sat forlornly on an altar outside the gates. Exactly two years prior, six militant Islamic terrorists, disguised as security forces, crept down the nearby hills and massacred a busload of European tourists, killing 62 people.

This might be a good time to talk about terrorists. The question that always comes to my mind is: *why?* Why do they hate us so passionately? After the bombing of the American embassy in New York in 1993, after the 1996 bombing of the Khobar Towers in Saudi Arabia, after Osama bin Laden declared *jihad*, holy war, on Americans in 1996, after the 1998 embassy bombings in East African capitals cities of Kenya, Tanzania, Dar es Salaam and Nairobi, after the 2000 attack on the USS Cole in Yemen, 911 still hit us blindside. Almost no one saw it coming. On September 12, 2001, me and 300 million Americans woke and asked ourselves: *Why?* What fanatical and fearless brand of thinking led 19 Arab men to board airplanes and turn them into torpedoes?

The answer is long and complicated, and impossible to capsulize. It confounds the American sense that the world is a fundamentally fair and hopeful place. I don't understand terrorism, or the tangles of Middle Eastern conflicts. (Can anyone, who hasn't inherited generations of lawless blood on both sides, understand it?) I only know what I've read, what has been told to me, what my heart tells me. And still I don't really understand it.

Religious fervor: Many fundamental Muslims believe that, as *infidels*, nonbelievers in Islam, Westerners are poisoning Arab lands and their people as surely as if we were passing out mustard gas on street corners. We're brash, reckless, and brazen sinners, leading believers off the true path to God. Osama bin Laden, in his declaration of *jihad* said, "Terrorizing you, while you are carrying arms on our land [meaning military instillations in Saudi Arabia], is a legitimate and morally demanded duty."

This is just one good reason for the separation of Church and State—a concept many Middle Eastern factions have never embraced. Fundamental Islamists consider westerners a cancerous infestation, which they must eradicate from their culture. They blame the decline of Muslim societies on western influences and foreign occupation.

Land: The conflicts aren't just ideological. Violent firestorms rage over control of land, ports, and oil, with the Arabs pitted against the Jews, and the Americans weighing in heavily (with foreign policy decisions, and military and financial aid) on the side of Israel.

In the minds of many Arabs, Israel and their American allies have bombed the crap out of them, funded and trained their enemies, occupied their land, humiliated, degraded, and tortured them. We've killed Arabs, the children of Arabs, and the hope of the Arab people.

History records the many bloody tales of Christian Crusaders fighting Arab armies for control of Jerusalem—the land that was holy to both nation states. Modern history begins somewhere between then and now.

Let's start in 1947 when the United Nations took 56% of Palestine— much of which was home to Arabs for centuries of time—and gave it to mournful and deserving Jewish refugees, who had been targeted, tortured, robbed and dislocated in WWII. The partition placed 36% of the existing Arab population inside a Jewish state. UN Resolution 181 was implemented against the wishes of the majority of the inhabitants affected by it. (Afghanistan, Cuba, Egypt, Greece, India, Iran, Iraq, Lebanon, Pakistan, Saudi Arabia, Syria, Turkey, and Yemen voted against the resolution.) War broke out immediately. The Jews won a decisive victory, expanded their state, and created several hundred thousand Palestinian refugees.

Resentments and bloodshed only grew. The Middle East became a world unto itself, sick with conflicts, punctuated by assassinations, terror and retaliation, leaving millions dead on all sides.

We call them terrorists. They call themselves resistance fighters. History will decide which was the evil empire, and which were the freedom fighters.

One in every five people in the world are Muslim, from all points of the globe— from Morocco to Indonesia, Kazakhstan to China, Bangladesh to Turkey, and including all the heavy hitters: Egypt, Iraq, Afghanistan, and Iran. Also Nigeria, India and Lebanon. And more.

America's agenda to make an oil grab in the Middle East and install the seed of democracy in Iraq was a miserable failure. Except for the oil part. In one case, it's worse than a failure. In late 2006, the *New York Times* reported that a National Intelligence Estimate attributed a direct role to the Iraq war in *fueling* terrorism. The report asserted that "the American invasion and occupation of Iraq has helped spawn a new generation of Islamic radicalism and that the overall terrorist threat has *grown* since the Sept. 11 attacks… Islamic radicalism, rather than being in retreat, has metastasized and spread across the globe."

Ironically, Islam is a religion of peace. The Koran says, "He who kills by design shall burn in Hell forever. He shall incur the wrath of God, who will lay His curse on him and prepare him for a woeful scourge." Also, "Whoever kills a human being shall be looked upon as though he had killed all mankind; and whoever saves a human life shall be regarded as though he had saved all mankind."

Still, radical "believers" are fighting the Western world with a violent combination of dogma, terrorism, and technology. (These terrorists are *not* ragtag hooligans living in caves and plotting the overthrow of Western Civilization like madmen. They are technologically advanced, well-funded and very, very determined.) They consider this a holy war in every aspect. We see them as demons. They see themselves as liberators, doing the work of God.

Generations of Arabs have been, and continue to be, born into violent conflicts on the streets of their cities and in their holy lands. Theirs is a generation of rage. Terrorism is their only shred of power, of retaliation, of voice, in a global stage of politics and economy that has marginalized and humiliated them for decades.

Thursday / November 18 / The Nile

Potato chips. They called them "chippies", and served them at the bar like peanuts, piled high as pyramids on salad plates. I loved them for that.

As the only loner on the ship—which isn't how cruises are done *at all*—I had the opportunity to make great friends with all the bartenders onboard: Mustafa, Muhammad and Khaled. They poured me wine, fed me potato chips and helped me with my Arabic. Muhammad offered to help me buy silver and gold goblets in Aswan or Cairo. Cheaper in Cairo, he said, and he gave me his number there. He'd be there on Sunday, he said, and I should call him up. I was sorry I wouldn't be able to.

All the staff members were as warm and friendly and as helpful as long-lost friends. They seemed to appreciate attempts at their language. I found myself wishing I could memorize more of it, but the words I taught myself kept slipping from my grasp, like fish I was trying to pull from the water by the nose.

Those days on the ship were easy compared to Cairo and Sinai. Almost too easy: tidy and self-contained. But it was a flat-out blessing to be relieved from solving problems minute by minute. The food was all included in the cruise fee, and was served in a generous combination of buffet and table service. To the tables they brought large trays of appetizers, figs, olives and cheeses. Salads, main courses and desserts were to be found on the buffet table. A 12 percent gratuity was added automatically to all the extras: beer, wine and bottled water. We tipped the servers on the ship, and all the rest was taken care of, on our behalf, by Sabre and his colleagues.

We docked at the port of Edfu and visited the Temple of Horus. This temple is one of the best preserved in Egypt, built under the direction of Cleopatra's Macedonian ancestors. This monument took over 180 years to build, its completion marking, roughly, Christ's 25 birthday.

After touring the temple, we walked through an outdoor bazaar and bought *jallabiyas* for that night's costume party on the ship. A *jallabiya* is a traditional, robe-type garment still worn by many Egyptian men, akin to a moo moo. I settled, instead, with something more akin to silk pajamas: wide pants and a white shirt.

Of course, there has to be a snake in this story. This one, a cobra, was lifting its menacing head from a little mat on the ground, at the coaxing of its handler. I stood at a discreet distance, repelled, entranced. I'd never seen a snake sweat before. It must have been tired, bored, and mercilessly overworked. I couldn't image crossing one's path in the desert: angry, well heeled and itching for a fight.

As I came to the steps to re-board the ship that night, I encountered a little girl selling cigarettes. She was pretty and dirty and small, seven or eight years old. I was playing with Barbie Dolls at that age. I'd never been alone on the street at her age, not once. I had a wrinkled Egyptian pound in my pocket and I pulled it out for her. Twenty-nine cents. I boarded the ship weary to the bone.

Sabre took us out every day, like kids on a field trip, and guided us through the temples and tombs of Upper Egypt. Sabre had a lisp and was hard to understand. He told us too much of one thing and nothing of so many others. He was arrogant and impatient and stomped his foot when other guides or tourists were talking too loud or getting too close to him. "Do you have someone responsible for you?" he demanded of two wandering Japanese visitors in the Valley of the Kings. Stomp. Stomp, stomp, stomp. "Quiet, please!" in the Temple of Karnak. I wanted him to translate the hieroglyphics and tell the stories of the ancient gods. "This is very important because..." "That is very important because..." I forgot everything he said.

I took a photograph of a statue of a falcon at Hatchepsut's temple. "It's not an original!" he scoffed. "Can't you tell?" Ummm ... No. Truth was, Sabre's knowledge was immense and his passion was great. I think maybe he should have been behind a desk in the Egyptian Museum, though—in a dark, quiet little office, cataloguing artifacts, where he could have antiquity all to himself.

He knew the crowds, though, and could rearrange our passage to best avoid them. He was a master of getting there first, and of rerouting the tour on a dime.

At the most popular monuments, hoards of tourists gather, each group following their guides like trusting little ducks. Sometimes the guides would compete for the next turn at an important waypoint, or the most strategic position in a temple. They offered each a strained politeness, and if I weren't a little duckling myself, following Sabre from one site to another, I would have stayed behind once or twice to see the Battle of the Guides played out.

In one case, I watched the Lady with the Umbrella versus the Man with the Walking Stick. (Each guide had his or her own rallying instrument—an umbrella, a clipboard, a colorful hat, something to hold high, around which their charges could recognize and flock.) In this case, Umbrella Woman got there first. But Walking Stick Man had a more strategic position. I had to go as they started jockeying for control by raising their voices and assuming the floor. It appeared that Walking Stick Man was winning, and as I left the area, I wondered if Umbrella Woman, weary herself, wouldn't just swear up an Arabic blue streak at him, as she moved her group to another station on the tour.

By now, America started disappearing in my mind. I couldn't remember words for simple things: scrapbook, for example. I dreaded going back to work and even as I wrote the words on the page, *Earth Year 2000*, they seemed foreign to me.

My last night on The Nile Romance I was busy writing in my journal and chatting with Muhammad at the bar.

"So, are you writing about me?" This from a stranger, well-dressed, slick, smelling of Old Spice.

"I don't think I know you." I turned back to my pages, consumed with the important business at hand: words. I didn't notice Muhammad's posture at the moment.

The same man approached me a little later. "So, am I in your book, yet?"

"I don't know you, yet."

"I'm Sharif, the captain of the ship."

"The *what?*"

"The captain."

"You are not." I looked to Muhammad for confirmation. On his best behavior, surrounded by other staff and guides, he nodded, *yes.*

"Pleased to meet you," I stammered, shaking his hand. Why wasn't he wearing a white uniform with gold epaulets on his shoulders, like Gavin MacLeod on "The Love Boat"? Wasn't that the least a captain should do? Instead, Sharif sat down and chatted with me for a long time. He drew me a map of Egypt, noting every city on a paper placemat. He promised he'd have the bright lights on the sundeck turned out that night so I could see the stars. And he offered me a tour of the bridge the next morning. He made a call on the telephone and then gave instructions to the staff standing nearby. Epaulets or not, this guy was in charge. "Muhammad will take you to the bridge, tomorrow at 8 A.M.," he announced. Then something important came up and he excused himself. "*Shokran, shokran.*"

That night I laid myself down, alone on the sundeck, and watched a zillion stars float by. The next morning, Muhammad took me to the bridge.

Here's the funny part: I was expecting the bridge to be large and decked out with men in those same white uniforms of my imagination. I expected a wooden steering wheel with spokes, and a big brass bell. No. The bridge was a narrow sliver at the front of the boat, with an ashtray on the console.

The pilot was wearing a gray *jallabiya* and a white cap on his head. There were shabby curtains hung on the windows and no place for the man to sit. The boat was steered by three joysticks, one for each engine. "Caterpillar," he announced proudly.

The pilot showed me each and every button on the console, and Muhammad translated its purpose and use. I smiled at every nob and nodded my head as if I understood. The setting was so modest, the pilot so proud in contrast, and Muhammad so good and earnest, I felt undeserving. When the invitation was extended to the engine room, I passed. My cup runneth over.

Muhammad and I were both gloomy as we went back to the bar. Muhammad proceeded to make me the singularly best cup of espresso with milk on the planet. *How did he do that?* Coffee in Egypt is unreasonably good. And in the absence of beer and wine, they drink a lot of it.

When it came time to say goodbye, I gave Muhammad a warm hug. "I give you a blessing," he said. And he kissed me on each cheek. I stood alone in the reception area with nothing to do but wait for my luggage. I had to put on my sunglasses; I was starting to cry.

Chapter Ten

Cairo: The Last Days

MAAT: *Maat is the personification of cosmic order, truth, justice and harmony. She and Thoth took part in the creation of the world and Maat is the world's moral compass. It is her feather that is weighed against the heart at the end of life. She is depicted as a woman wearing an ostrich feather on her head.*

I had three days left before American Airlines took me back over the Atlantic Ocean to "real life." I didn't want to go. I hadn't seen every thing I wanted to see; I had seen too much of others. If I could stay in Egypt, I thought I could stay *special*. Back home, I was no one. I was nothing. As long as I stayed in Egypt, I could be whoever I wanted to be.

This was a lie. But I was happy to be telling it to myself as my journey drew to a close.

Saturday / November 20 / Nile Hilton

Tarak smiled when he saw me and shook my hand. My favorite bartender in Cairo already knew: red wine, please. "You are better than the last time I saw you," he said. "I know your eyes. Last time they were red."

I cried a lot in Egypt. Mostly about the children. I also harbored this crazy idea that I would return to Egypt with some sexy, brilliant photographer and together we would write a beautiful book about the children of the Egypt. We would travel to the cities and the remote villages and the farms and I would tell their stories and people would read them and things would change. People would stop calling Arabs "towel heads," for one thing, and their hearts would empty themselves of hate—because they would realize that terrorism is not the soul of these people. No more than Timothy McVeigh, who bombed the Federal Building in Oklahoma City in 1995, was the soul of America. Most Muslims are ordinary, innocent people, just like us.

I would tell the stories of the children. I would tell these stories:

The young boy at the Khan al-Kahlili bazaar, who carried a crate on his slender back through the traffic and throngs of people on dirt streets. He didn't notice me, but I remember him. Children will do anything their parents ask them, I suppose. Did he realize it wasn't fair? Did he know that he was too young and his burden was too heavy?

The three little children sleeping on cardboard on a cement walkway in Old Cairo. Their mother was sadly holding out her hand, too weary of poverty and hunger to beg out loud. I passed them by and ten steps later returned and handed her three pounds, less than a dollar. "For the children," I mumbled. I pointed with my eyes, too flooded to see clearly, and turned and walked away.

The pretty, poor, dirty little girl under the lamplight at the Port of Kom Ombo. The one selling cigarettes who made me think of Barbie Dolls. I wanted to take her with me, put her in a bubble bath, clean and comb her hair, and tuck her away from the lonely streets into a pink canopy bed.

The little boy in a hand-made boat, paddling all alone on the Nile up to passengers in *fellucas* (sail boats). He sang songs in four different languages for *baksheesh*. Baksheesh, I was told, means to share. Not, "give me money, please," but rather, "share your wealth." The distinction is important.

The many young boys outside the papyrus store in Aswan, selling bookmarkers at a pound a piece. Their wares were wrinkled and worn from being held all day in sweaty little fists and then spread into fans like a deck of cards for your viewing pleasure. They were relentless and I bought too many and paid too much. But they smiled and let me take their pictures. When I left, I blew them kisses from my seat on the air-conditioned bus as they stood in the glaring heat, dealing cheap papyrus to an endless stream of tourists.

The Bedouin boys selling egg-shaped rocks and rock-shaped rocks and perfect-fitting split-apart rocks with crystal surprises inside. I let them use my camera. I wished I'd brought a Polaroid, so I could have given each one a picture of himself. Maybe something for them to look back on from better, easier times to come.

The lucky little girls in blue dresses and white scarves, all matching, walking arm in arm through the streets to school. Theirs was the next generation, the next chance for change, and hope. I wondered if maybe the West and the Middle East would be friends by the time they grew up. Maybe they would throw off those scarves some day. Maybe not.

The Aswan boy who over-sold me cigarettes and gave me his lighter with a knowing smile between the cheated and the cheater. I later gave that same yellow lighter as *baksheesh* to a man who sold me three silk scarves. I didn't have a pen to give him so I gave him the lighter. For some incomprehensible reason, everyone on those streets wanted a Bic.

The little Nubian boy at the boat dock on Philae who insisted I buy three necklaces that smelled of spice and dangled small slices of dried coconut. Three for a pound. Ten cents a piece. They stained my hand purple. They ended up in the first waste receptacle I came to, but I can smell those necklaces still.

All the children I said no to, when I could just as easily have said yes.

The many children and their teachers at the pyramids who just wanted to have their pictures taken with me, and to tell me their names. I repeated each one as best as I could.

The little boy in a green T-shirt who was riding down the road in the most unusual, unlikely and ingenious combination of donkey, rope and barrel. I don't think that the world has ever seen such a contraption, before or since. But it did the trick, and was a testimony to the human imagination.

The girl with the water bottle at the Coptic museum. Smile, click, thank you. This is how a nine-year-old makes a living.

I remember the children of Egypt. They're taped and glued and tucked into the haphazard scrapbook of my memories. They're out there, right now, right this minute, carrying the burden of their parents, like crates on their slender backs.

Sunday / November 21 / Cairo

Amr checked me into the most luxurious hotel in Cairo and met me in the deli for coffee. (I tell you, Starbucks needs to go to Egypt for some extensive research.) We sat for two hours with each other, just visiting. When I was young, I would often go with my grandmother to her friend's or a relative's house, to visit. God, it was boring. What was this "visiting" all about? Who cares? Can't we go outside and play? "Visits" were interminable. I thought they were the kiss of death. But I was young. What did I know?

Among other things, Amr and I talked about money. We talked about wealthy men of the world—who buy and sell commodities—trading money and properties but never *making* anything. Except more money. "Who are you?" asked Amr. "If you buy it and keep it and sell it for a higher price, you have made money. But you have not contributed something good. Who are you?" Amr talked of using money to make a business—creating jobs for people, increasing what you do, increasing jobs as you go. He spoke of philanthropy, not to have your name emblazoned on a building, but to give something to people. To build a hospital or equip the needy. To build homes for homeless people. "Who are you just to make money?" he said. "You are nothing."

Charity, it turns out, is one of the five pillars of Islam, which include: *Shahadah*, the testimony of faith, *Salat*, ritual prayer five times a day, *Zakat*, obligatory almsgiving, *Siyam*, fasting, and *Hajj*, the pilgrimage to Mecca once in a lifetime. Muslims typically give, by religious law, 2.5% of their general wealth to charity. This money is given to both religious and secular institutions: mosques, schools, hospitals, programs for the poor, and programs for women, orphans and communities in need.

You must hide your left hand, though, so it does not see what you are giving. If the left hand knows what the right hand has done, it won't be secret. And the gift could be advertised for propaganda or self-recognition. (Like your name plastered on a hospital wing, or a college football stadium, for example.) No, it must be given in compassion for the less fortunate, and not for recognition. Also, during *Ramadan*, Muslims fast until sundown, so they understand what it is to be hungry. And to have compassion.

"And be steadfast in your prayer and pay charity," says the Qur'an 2:110. "Whatever good you send forth for your future, you shall find it with God, for God is well aware of what you do."

Now there's a thought. Is God well aware of me? And everything I do? I wondered this, because, since Sinai, He seemed to have retreated again to busier matters. God didn't keep company with me. We didn't "visit." He seemed to appear in small moments of inspiration, rather, shining a light on me and then disappearing again. Did he notice things, like my grandmother used to? Moments when I felt invisible and hurt, was He watching me?

When I was 13 years old, I had an evil stepsister named Elaine. We lived in Seattle, at the time, with my dad and evil stepmother, Arlene. One summer—before that marriage busted up and my dad unwittingly came home to a house that had been cleaned out and loaded into a U-Haul—Elaine went with my brother, Ken, and me to my grandparent's cabin on Ashby Creek in Montana. She talked me into doing this weird acrobatic trick—note: she was much bigger than I was—with me sitting on her shoulders, bending backward while she held onto my feet, and landing in a handstand on the ground. I landed on my collarbone instead, fracturing the slender stick that holds my arm in place. "I don't want to play anymore," I said, and quietly took myself to the creek. I sat myself down on the bridge, and dangled my feet in the water. My grandmother didn't see the handstand fiasco, but she saw me on the bridge, just sitting there. She knew instantly that something was wrong.

Was God watching me this closely? Did He know, even before I did, how hurt I was? Or that I was in trouble? Or suffering? Could He pick me up, drive me to town, and take me in for spiritual X-rays? Could He wrap a brace around my fractured heart and heal me up? He took my Gramma from me years prior, when He gave her mind to Alzheimer's, and I'd felt alone ever since.

I'm not a person who blames God for everything that goes wrong in my life. But I wish He'd help me clean up the mess once in awhile. In His defense, however, I don't always bother to ask. In my most lucid moments, I can see His handiwork all through my life, and the many blessings I've been given.

I was here, after all, in Egypt, making new friends and new memories. I was learning gratitude and its great power to heal what is broken. I was walking out of the long dark halls of despair into the warm light of day. I may have had a bumpy start in life, a rough take-off, and some devastating turbulence, but I knew love, great love. And if that isn't the touch of God's hand, what is?

Monday / November 22 / Semiramas Intercontinental Hotel

Someone lit up my heart every day in Egypt. Every single day. This day it was Yasser, who sold me an alabaster bowl on the floor of the hotel gift store. I had a long list of presents to bring back to the states and I was still one short. So, though I had systematically avoided the finer gift stores in favor of local shopkeepers, I had one hour on my last night in Egypt to find one more thing.

So there I was, sitting on the floor of a deserted, swanky store in the finest hotel in Cairo, trying to pick out a bowl for my Grampa, who likes candy. The sales clerk, Yasser, joined me on the floor, and showed me about a hundred pieces of pottery.

Shokran, I said as we went along, as I rejected piece after piece in my search for the perfect candy dish.

"You speak Arabic?" Yasser asked.

"No. Only a few words."

"What words?"

I recited all the Arabic I knew: *Manfadlak, ma'as salama, aiwa, afwan, la, Allah wa Akbar, ahlan, sadik, in shaa Allah,* and *be kaam da*. Please, good-bye, yes, God is great, you're welcome, no, hello, friend, God willing, and how much. Not a particularly impressive showing for two weeks' time. But Yasser taught me more:

Salam ale kom, and in response, *ale kom el Salem*. Peace be upon you. And also with you.

Antei asmik eh? What is your name?

Ana asmi. My name is Kyla (اليك).

Da kifaya. That's enough. I'm finished. (Might have come in handy with some little bookmarker merchants I know in Aswan.)

"You are like us Egyptians," said Yasser. "You smile. And you speak Arabic."

Then Yasser wrote my name in hieroglyphics : A basket for K, two feathers for Y, a lion for L, and an eagle for A. The basket, I'm happy to report, means I'm very smart, wanting to try many things. The feathers are for justice and indicate a lovely person. The lion represents a strong person, who likes to be the boss and in control. "It means you have a good heart," Yasser explained. "You will be very strong with your husband," he added, and we both laughed. The eagle indicated that I have good character and protect myself well. That I value the freedom to fly and will travel many places.

I was happy that the letter for whatever symbol means stupid, lazy, cruel and arrogant, wasn't in my name.

I finally picked a stunning bowl of the palest yellow alabaster, with a lid inlaid with mother-of-pearl, to keep the dust off Grampa's candy. I said a long good-bye to Yasser. As I walked away, I found myself wishing—as I had so many times before in Egypt—that I could reach into my pocket and offer him something special. Something more than Egyptian pounds.

The river out the window of my room was the Nile. Sometimes I had to remind myself of that. I'd become accustomed to it, forgetting that I was in the company of one of the mightiest rivers on the globe. As I looked out over the Nile on that last day in Cairo, I fervently hoped to return again some day. Part of me wanted not to leave at all. Could I do it? Could I just *not go back?* I thought for about one millisecond that it was actually possible. That I could just turn my back on my friends and my family and my sorrows, and start over with a clean slate, a *tabula rasa*, a tablet scraped clean. I thought—through the grace of God and a little courage—I could reinvent myself in Egypt.

I was sitting on the Corniche at that moment, listening to car horns, watching people stroll along, seeing the last rays of light glisten on the river. I realized that the sun was just then rising on my home in Oregon, ten hours of daylight away. It gave me comfort to think of it—how the day was just beginning for my friends and family and how happy we would be when that same sun shined on us together.

The pages of my journal were nearly full and my great adventure was drawing itself down with the setting sun. My life back home had seemed so ordinary and small this whole time. I knew when I went back that I wouldn't have to try so hard at everything, and that the people I encountered would not be so gracious to me. Perhaps we were all the same, though—and that people were earnest and helpful and lighthearted—and I just didn't see home that way until I left it behind.

I thought about all the people I met and saw there—British, Spanish, French, Israeli, Indian, Arab, Philippine, Japanese, and German—all intermingling in the home of the Egyptians. The Muslims and the Christians, the Copts and the Jews, and those who have no God, had gathered together in this ancient land. For some purpose, they had each come here, and had made the world smaller.

"I will miss Egypt," I had told Amr earlier that day, as we sat drinking thick Turkish coffee on a patio overlooking el-Tarir Square.

"Egypt will miss you, too," he said. Outrageous as it sounds, I believed him.

Epilogue
America: Clean and Easy

ANUBIS: *Anubis, depicted as a man with a jackal's head, presides over funerary rites. In the presence of 42 assessor gods, Anubis weighs the deceased's heart against Maat's feather of truth. This determines the quality of one's life, and whether the soul will ascend to eternity or be devoured.*

I came back to America just as Madison Avenue and every big-box store and retail chain in the country was launching their biggest push of the year: Black Friday. With Christmas right around the corner, America was deluged with twinkling lights, provocative commercials, and all the newest, best, high-end, can't-live-without-them products on every shelf. I was re-embraced by the familiar and the ordinary: good mannered traffic, the English language, money I didn't have to multiply by .341, and *The Simpsons.*

I found myself longing to return to Egypt. I wanted to go back where everything was real and raw and unpredictable. America seemed awful to me: commercial, shallow, vain and self-indulgent. I had traveled through some invisible, cultural decompression chamber over the Atlantic, and now I was ordinary again.

Tuesday / February 20, 2013 / Bend, Oregon, USA

It's my 54th birthday. More than 13 years have passed since I went to Egypt. I was forty years old then. I learned a lot about myself on that journey. I had more confidence, an expanded view of God and my place in the Universe, and a greater appreciation for different cultures.

The suffocating weight of sorrow over the loss of my grandmother and Terry was lightening. People used to tell me that I have to let go of the dead. I looked at these people as if there were screaming lunatics. I didn't want to let go. I wanted to keep my loved ones close. I wanted them to come back to me. As my life moved on, it seemed increasingly cruel and unfair that they weren't here, too, on earth, living and breathing and being happy again. My happiness seemed linked to theirs.

Little by little, though. I did let them go, mostly. I still get blue and restless every November. I put a bronze star around my neck and hike into the Oregon woods, to the secret spot Terry revealed to me on the McKenzie River. This place gave him comfort, he once told me, where the world didn't seem so hard.

I still find myself, in moments, with an intense longing for my grandmother. I want desperately to hold her silky soft hands again, to see her watery, pale blue eyes, and to tell her how much I love her.

It crosses my mind occasionally and intensely—as perfectly fair and logical—that I have paid my penance: I have let them go. And now I should be able to have them back.

Finally, as my Gramma would have wished for me, I let myself find happiness. Mostly.

When I was forty-four, I married Mike—a tall, dark, handsome, brilliant, radioman. He managed radio stations in Central Oregon and I ran a magazine. He was meat and potatoes; I was salads and sushi. He listened to Rush Limbaugh; I listened to NPR. He played racquetball; I played tennis. I was clingy and talkative; he was the strong, silent type. We were opposites in every conceivable way. We were inseparable. But our marriage was doomed.

We tried to have babies after we got married, but it was too late. After two years, two tries and $30,000, we gave up. I was crushed beyond bearing. When I learned that my eggs were too old to conceive my own children, I roamed our house like a phantom for two solid days, walking in circles, dragging my hands through my hair, crying in despair.

My greatest regret was that all that was the best of me, the good that I had inherited from my grandparents and my parents and the heartiest of my ancestors, would be gone. There were other grandchildren to carry on what was great and amazing about those who came before them, but I was dead to this world. My parents had a cumulative total of zero grandchildren to carry on their genes, I'm sorry to say. My father had only two children, Ken and me, and neither of us had kids of our own. My mother had four children in her lifetime, by three husbands, and none of those children had children, either.

My darling Grampa died on April 5, 2004, three days short of his 80th birthday, and ten years after his wife died. I like to believe that he has arrived at gentler shores than the lonely life he lived after Gramma died. I like to believe he's living happily with her right now, somewhere on the banks of Ashby Creek.

I've spent some time cycling. Road bike, skinny tires, long distances, big hills, sweet downhill flights.

I was grinding up a long ride along the Cascade Lakes Scenic Highway the other day, approaching the top of an interminable, hot, climb—out of water, legs aching, wheezing for air. Several switchbacks stood between the looming distance to the top and me. Spinning, spinning, endlessly spinning.

Just about the time I seriously wanted to give up, I started to imagine that someone dark and threatening—a saboteur on fast wheels—was trying to pass me. I wanted to stop, get off, surrender to the merciless forces of doubt and gravity, and push my bike to the top, limping and dragging my tired bones in an act of unmitigated surrender. Better: I should just stop, lay in the soft green grass, and call for transport to the comfort of my air-conditioned home.

Then I imagined a cadre of supporters, echoing in my ear: *Don't you give up.* They pushed me from behind, these angels of heaven and earth. They gave life to my aching muscles. They breathed air into my lungs. And I pushed on.

Near the top, I could start to make out this ethereal gathering of heroes, lining the roadway on either side. *What was that sound?* Cheering! A chorus of encouragement, hollering out their belief in me, with their ever-present support. There stood Terry, Gramma, Grampa, Dad, sister Raine, brother Ken. Brenda, Tami, Ande, Jennifer (best friends of all time). In the far distance, Pat, Ben, Mike, Gary, Clark (the best lover ever—*sigh*), my Sunday school teachers (with their hankies tucked into the sleeves of their paisley dresses), my college drama coach—everyone who ever loved me or rejected me. *Go! Go! Go! Come on, Kyla! You can do it!* All jumping up and down for me, smiling, hugging each other. Cheering me to the top, to the Finish Line.

This scenario came from nothing more than my imagination. Something from nothing. My imagination has that power. *Your* imagination has that power. To imagine is to create. To create is given from our Creator. Our imagination plugs us into to a direct line with the Universe. When you have nothing, something is a gift. From God/Universe/Spirit/Source, call it what you will. It is real and powerful. It gets you through the switchbacks and up the long interminable, desperate climbs that take us out of the darkest corners of our despair and to the highest peaks of our endeavors. That's what I believe, anyway. And it gets me through.

The Finish Line still eludes me, but I climb on. I climb. I am not, not ever, alone.

After 911, the notion of going back to Egypt seemed impossible. Too much had changed. By the time news broke of torture at Abu Graib, Amr and I had stopped exchanging emails. I didn't know what to say to him anymore.

Still, though, I hear Egypt calling my name from time to time. I smell the smoky scent of roasted meat and I smell jasmine in the salty air. I see the Nile swish calmly by and I hear the call of the *Muezzin*. I feel the kiss of friendship on my cheek and I taste the red wine at Tarak's bar.

Maybe, after all, time on this earth is all we have of value. What is the measure of a person's life? Why will people give so much of themselves just to share time with a traveling stranger? For all the places and adventures, the strange and exotic things, the question arises in me: does it all come down to time, and with whom we spend it? Is place inextricably linked to our experience of other people and ourselves? How far will a woman go to satisfy her need to be connected to the people and the land of this earth?

When Dorothy came back from Oz, she realized that everything important to her was right where she left it: at home. But there are those of us for whom this is simply not true.

We belong on the Yellow Brick Road. We carry our homes in our hearts. What we bring back from our days, what we leave behind, becomes the story of our lives.

Are we running away? Or are we running toward the heart of love— our one true home? Maybe I'll understand some day. In the mean time, I belong to the road.

THE END

ACKNOWLEDGEMENTS

SESHAT: *Seshat was the divine measurer and scribe who recorded, by notching her palm, the time allotted to the pharaoh for his stay on earth. She was depicted with a stylized, sevenpoint papyrus above her head. She wears a dress of cheetah or leopard print. Seshat recorded the actions of all people on the leaves of the sacred Persea tree.*

Everything remotely good in my character came to me from my grandparents, Bob and Effie Morris, who raised me and loved me and taught me how to fish. My Gramma also taught me how to sew and knit and build a fire—which later in life seemed dorky compared to kids who were raised with music and ballet lessons, until I realized that you can't cook s'mores on a grand piano. In the care of my grandparents, I played dress-up in alligator pumps and silk paisley dresses from rummage sales, in the coolest backyard playhouse on the block. I played make-believe and incubated my imagination in the warm light of their love. I played pinochle on Friday nights when my high school peers were out running amuck. I listened to stories of the olden days. I learned how to laugh until my sides hurt. I owe them everything.

My Dad insisted that I go to college all those years ago, even though it wasn't necessarily Merwin-esque at the time to do so. He paid my way through that adventure and though many haps and mishaps since then. Without his love and support, I'd probably be a bag lady right now. In any case, I wouldn't have had the opportunities I did. As a Coug at Washington State University, for example, I learned how to be a restless underdog year after year, and then pop up out of nowhere and kick some serious bootie.

If Jim Prather hadn't hired me as a revenue consultant at Ceridian for a short stint in 1999, at a spectacular hourly rate, I could not have afforded to leave for Egypt in the first place. He and his wife, Mary, have been second parents and friends to me since I was a gangly grade-schooler.

A woman's girlfriends become her anchors in this turbulent life, slapped around as we may become by happenstance and fate. I am no exception. The one thing I know every day is that Brenda Barnes, Jennifer Straughan, Sonya Westerman, Tami Elliot, and Ande Cardwell love me. And I love them.

My writing associate, couch mate, travel companion and snuggle bunny is Pippin, the Golden-on-the-Go. My only regret about Pip is that he doesn't know how much he comforts my restless heart.

To the readers who embark with me on this journey: *thank you*. I write the story, the best I can, of the generosity and warmth of the Egyptian people, the travelers I met, the pharaohs, the preachers and the politics, the ancient stones of time, and the children who work so very hard. Welcome to the great adventure on the other side of fear.

My wish for you is this:

Go places.
Follow your heart.
Tell the truth.
Have the time of your life.

CPSIA information can be obtained at www.ICGtesting.com
Printed in the USA
BVOW05s2150050614

355559BV00001B/1/P